Rebecca Parkinson lives in Lan[...] two children. Since graduating [...] [...]ity, she has worked as a teacher, [...] [...]er for science, university lecturer and course [...]tor. At present, Rebecca teaches part-time in a primary school while pursuing her career in writing. She is the author of over 20 books.

Rebecca is part of the leadership team at her local Free Methodist Church, where, along with her husband, she runs the youth and children's work, and has also been involved in projects working with teachers in local schools and youth clubs in other counties. In her spare time she enjoys sport, especially badminton and kayaking. Rebecca's first resource book, *Fill the Gap!*, was published by Barnabas for Children in 2012.

Text copyright © Rebecca Parkinson 2015
The author asserts the moral right to be identified as the author of this work

Published by
The Bible Reading Fellowship
15 The Chambers, Vineyard
Abingdon OX14 3FE
United Kingdom
Tel: +44 (0)1865 319700
Email: enquiries@brf.org.uk
Website: www.brf.org.uk
BRF is a Registered Charity

ISBN 978 0 85746 023 3

First published 2015
10 9 8 7 6 5 4 3 2 1 0

Acknowledgements

Unless otherwise stated, scripture quotations are taken from the Holy Bible, New International Version. Scriptures quoted from the Good News Bible published by The Bible Societies/HarperCollins Publishers Ltd, UK © American Bible Society 1966, 1971, 1976, 1992, used with permission.

Cover photo: © Andersen Ross: Getty Images

Every effort has been made to trace and contact copyright owners for material used in this resource. We apologise for any inadvertent omissions or errors, and would ask those concerned to contact us so that full acknowledgement can be made in the future.

A catalogue record for this book is available from the British Library

Printed and bound by CPI Group (UK) Ltd, Croydon CR0 4YY

HELP!

IT'S THE ALL-AGE
SLOT

52 instant
talk outlines
for church services

For the people at Ashton Baptist Church, Preston, who made my childhood experiences of church so special.

Acknowledgements

As a child and young person I was fortunate to have many people who worked hard to make church a wonderful place to be. I would like to thank them for everything they did and for the difference they made to my life and the lives of many others.

As an adult it has been a privilege to share the love they showed in a wide variety of schools and churches. I would like to thank all the children and young people with whom I have worked for the joy they have given me.

Thanks as always to Ted, Anna and Lydia, for all their ideas and encouragement.

A special thanks to my mum and dad for their belief in me and their constant encouragement.

CONTENTS

☆ INTRODUCTION ☆

If you have ever been asked to lead an all-age service or prepare a children's or youth talk, or are simply in need of fresh ideas for assemblies and RE lessons, then this is the book for you.

Help! It's the All-Age Slot provides all-age talks that are not only easy to prepare but will also grip the entire congregation. The ideas are designed to be quick and easy to use and are clearly presented, with relevant Bible passages suggested. Each session has been tried and tested by children's and youth workers and will help to explain the Bible in a clear and stimulating manner.

There are 52 ready-made sessions, one for every week of the year. Some sessions relate to particular seasons in the church year, but most of them can be used at any point in the calendar. The material covers not only Christmas and Easter but also other significant Christian festivals such as Pentecost, Ascension, Harvest, Bible Sunday and All Saints Day. For each of these festivals, the Appendix lists the set Bible readings from the Lectionary, allowing for easy insertion of the readings into the church service.

All of these talks are suitable for use across the age ranges and are suitable for both smaller and larger groups. Where possible, it is hoped that they will be used to involve children and young people. For large groups, there may be occasions when it would be helpful to duplicate some of the suggested pieces of equipment so that more people can be actively involved.

A number of the talks require the involvement of two or more people. On these occasions, pre-planning is particularly important.

Each slot is designed to take between 10 and 15 minutes, although they can be easily shortened where necessary.

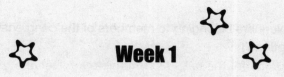

Week 1

WHAT A PLAN!

Aim
To illustrate that God has an amazing plan for our lives

Bible links

- Jeremiah 29:11 (God's plans for us)
- Psalm 31:15 (Our times are in God's hands)
- Proverbs 16:9 (God establishes our steps)
- Ephesians 2:10 (Planned good work)

You will need

- A blank calendar, large enough to be seen clearly from the front
- A list of dates through the year that would be considered important to people of different ages in the congregation (for example, school holidays, World Cup, Olympics, birthdays, wedding anniversaries)
- Pens
- A variety of calendars to introduce the talk (optional)

- Calendars belonging to members of the congregation (optional)

Talk outline

Ask the children if any of them received calendars for Christmas. Ask the congregation if they received calendars and see who received the most: people in business may have received several from clients. Point out that calendars are made in lots of shapes and sizes. Some have pop groups featured on them; some have other famous people or places or animals. Ask the congregation what features on their calendars and show them the selection you have brought.

If you have borrowed calendars from people in the congregation, ask those volunteers to stand at the front. Show the children the calendars and see if they can match the calendars to the correct people.

Show the congregation your large blank calendar. Ask someone to come to the front to have a look at the calendar and see if they can tell you why it isn't much use at the moment. If they don't notice, ask someone else to help them. If neither notices, begin to give clues such as, 'I know I have a dentist's appointment. Can you tell me when it is?' or 'I can't wait to go away on holiday! When is it that I am going?' Eventually someone will notice that there is nothing recorded on the calendar.

Ask for volunteers to write some important dates on to the calendar for you. For example, invite a child to mark the next school holiday and count how many more weeks or days they still have at school. Tell the congregation that you are having a weekend away on a certain date and ask someone to mark it on. Remind people that it is an elderly member's birthday next week and mark it on.

Ask the children if they think that calendars are important, and why. Explain that most things in our lives need to be planned. We need to plan what we are going to eat: the food doesn't just appear on the table. We need to plan where we are going on holiday: we can't just arrive somewhere and expect a room to be ready for us. We can't just decide which days we want to go to school and not turn up on all the other days. Birthdays, Christmas, days out, going to the cinema—all need planning.

The Bible tells us that God has plans for our lives. Our lives aren't an accident; God actually knew that we would be born. Even before we began to grow, God knew what we would look like and what he wanted us to do. In Ephesians 2:10 it says, 'We are God's handiwork, created in Christ Jesus to do good works, which God prepared in advance for us to do.' God has already prepared good things for us to do. Isn't that amazing?

Read Jeremiah 29:11: '"For I know the plans I have for you," declares the Lord, "plans to prosper you and not to harm you, plans to give you hope and a future."'

Point out that God's plans for us are always good. When things go wrong and we go through tough times, it's easy to think that God doesn't care. However, God's plans for our lives are always to prosper us and not to harm us. He always wants us to have hope.

Challenge

Challenge the congregation to write the verse from Jeremiah at the top of each month on their calendars. In that way, they can be reminded every day that God has an amazing plan for their lives and that he is with them in everything that they do.

Remind the congregation about Ephesians 2:10. Ask them to look actively for 'good works' this week, knowing that God has already prepared some things that he wants them to do.

Week 2

SPECIAL PRESENTS

Aim

To look at the significance of the gifts given
by the wise men at Epiphany

Bible links

- Matthew 2:1–12 (The wise men's visit)
- Revelation 17:14; 19:16 (King of kings)
- Hebrews 9:12; John 3:16; 1 John 2:2 (Sacrifice)
- Hebrews 4:14–15 (High priest)
- Mark 15:23 (Jesus on the cross)
- John 19:39 (Jesus' burial)
- 1 Peter 3:18 (Jesus' death)

You will need

- Four large boxes wrapped up as presents, each
  containing items suitable for different groups within the
  congregation (for example, baby clothes, toys, football,
  make-up, power tool, and so on)
- Three jars to represent gold, frankincense and myrrh

Talk outline

Ask some of the children to say what their favourite Christmas presents were. (This talk works well if the children have been asked to bring a present with them to show during the service.) Ask questions such as, 'Why do you think someone bought you that?' or 'Why do you like this present so much?'

Point out that people generally try to buy us presents that they know we will like. If we like a particular series of books, someone may buy us another in the series. If we like a particular type of chocolate, people will often buy us that type.

Show the four presents and explain that the labels have fallen off the presents, so you need some help giving them out. Explain that we need to see what is inside the parcels so that we can decide who might like the present. Ask for a volunteer to unwrap the first present. Show the congregation what is inside and ask the children what sort of person would want a present like this. For example, if the present is a baby's toy, pretend to give it to an adult in the congregation and ask if it would be suitable for them. If the present is a power tool, pretend to give it to a small child and ask if it would be a good present for them. Ask for the reasons why.

Do the same with the other three presents. Mention again that we give people gifts that are suitable for them. Point out that after Christmas Day, when we are clearing up, we often place our presents in piles. If we were to look at the pile of presents that each person received, it would tell us something about that person.

Read Matthew 2:1–12 or tell the story of the visit of the wise men to Jesus. Show the three jars and explain that each of the gifts that Jesus was given had a special meaning. Gold showed that Jesus was a king. At the time, Jesus didn't appear to be a king: he was born in a stable and placed to sleep in a manger. However, the Bible goes on to describe Jesus as the King of kings and the Lord of lords (Revelation 17:14; 19:16). The gift of gold was a symbol of what was to come.

Frankincense was a special perfume used by a priest. One of the priest's duties in the Bible was to make sacrifices to God, to make peace between God and the people for the wrong things that they had done. When Jesus died, he became the ultimate sacrifice for the wrong that we had done (Hebrews 9:12; John 3:16; 1 John 2:2). In the book of Hebrews, Jesus is described as the great high priest: Hebrews 4:14–15 says, 'Therefore, since we have a great high priest who has ascended into heaven, Jesus the Son of God, let us hold firmly to the faith we profess. For we do not have a high priest who is unable to feel sympathy for our weaknesses, but we have one who has been tempted in every way, just as we are—yet he did not sin.'

Myrrh was used to anoint the body of someone who had died. Myrrh is mentioned twice more in connection with Jesus. In Mark 15:23, as Jesus is crucified, he is offered wine mixed with myrrh, which he refuses to take. Then, in John 19:39, Nicodemus is seen to mix myrrh with other ingredients to place on Jesus' body before placing him in the tomb. The fact that the wise men gave Jesus myrrh right at the start of his life was a symbol that, one day, his death would be of great significance. Read 1 Peter 3:18: 'For Christ also suffered once for sins, the righteous for the unrighteous, to bring you to God.'

Gold represents a king, frankincense shows that Jesus would have an important role as a priest, and myrrh foretold that his death would have great significance. What an amazing collection of presents!

Challenge

Point out that the word 'Epiphany' comes from a Greek word meaning 'make something known'. When Jesus was born into the world, God began to 'make known' and to carry out the plan that had been promised for thousands of years. As people enjoy the presents they have received at Christmas, challenge them to think about the greatest present that has ever been given—the gift of Jesus.

Week 3

WHAT CAN YOU DO?

Aim
To illustrate that God can do more than we can ever imagine

Bible links

- Ephesians 3:20 (More than our imaginations)
- Matthew 19:26 (With God all things are possible)
- Matthew 10:30; Luke 12:7 (The hairs on our heads are numbered)

You will need

- A small cup of pasta
- A bag of rice
- A bucket of sand
- A picture of stars

Talk outline

Announce that you know there are many talented people in the room. Point out that you can see that many of them are fit and healthy, many of them are intelligent and many of them can do amazing things. Explain that you want to give people a few challenges that they may find difficult.

- Challenge 1: Ask for a volunteer who is willing to try to do something that most of the population cannot do. Once the volunteer is at the front, ask them to touch their nose with their elbow. (If you are in the unfortunate position of choosing someone who can actually do this, you may wish to ask for another volunteer.) Ask other members of the congregation to try it. Say that, while there are a few particularly flexible people who can do it, most of us will never be able to, no matter how hard we try.

- Challenge 2: Ask for a different volunteer and ask them to try to touch their chin or nose with their tongue. Explain that most of the congregation will never be able to do this, no matter how hard they try or how much they practise.

- Challenge 3: Ask if any of the children are good at counting. Ask for a volunteer to count the pieces of pasta in the cup. You may want to ask for two volunteers so that they can help each other. (Choose older children who will be good at counting.) Once the children have successfully completed the task, congratulate them before announcing that you were just checking that they could count well, as now you want them to do the real challenge. Give the children the bag of rice and, when they look shocked, ask them if they think this task is possible. Ask the congregation what they think. Now give the children the bucket of sand and ask them to count the grains. Ask other people if they think this would be possible. If they say it is possible, then ask if it would be possible to count all the grains of sand on the sea shore. Point out that this is definitely impossible.

Ask the children if anyone can guess how many stars there are in the sky, according to scientists. Tell them that there are millions and millions: even the best astronomers can't count how many.

Ask for a volunteer with long hair to come to the front. Ask if anyone thinks they would be able to count the volunteer's strands of hair. If someone volunteers to try, they will soon find that it is impossible.

Explain that the Bible tells us that although things are often impossible for us, nothing is impossible for God. Matthew 19:26 says, 'With God all things are possible.' Ask someone to read Matthew 10:30: 'Even the very hairs of your head are all numbered.' This task may be impossible for us to do, but God knows the answer.

Explain that Matthew 10:30 is found in a passage of the Bible where Jesus is telling the disciples that they needn't be afraid. Jesus was explaining that God knows absolutely everything about us, so we don't need to worry or be afraid in any situation.

Ask if any of the children have good imaginations. Ask them to share the most amazingly fantastic ideas they can imagine. Point out that sometimes we put limits on what we think God can do. Read Ephesians 3:20: 'Now to him who is able to do immeasurably more than all we ask or imagine…' God can't just do a tiny bit more than we can imagine. He can do so much more that we can never even measure it.

Challenge

Remind the congregation that, even when we feel as if there is no way through a situation, even when things seem to be going badly wrong, God can do things that we think are impossible. Read Ephesians 3:20–21: 'Now to him who is able to do immeasurably more than all we ask or imagine, according to his power that is at work within us, to him be glory in the church and in Christ Jesus throughout all generations, for ever and ever! Amen.' This was true in the time when the book of Ephesians was written, it is true today and it will be true for ever.

Challenge the congregation to read Ephesians 3:14–21 before they go to sleep tonight. Suggest that they might use it as a prayer, to pray for someone they know.

Week 4

ENGRAVINGS

Bible links

- Isaiah 49:15 (Never forgotten)
- Isaiah 49:16 (Engraved on his hands)
- John 20:24–30 (Jesus' pierced hands)

You will need

- A prearranged volunteer whose name is engraved on to an object (for example, jewellery, trophy, door plaque). It is important that this is a definite engraving, which cannot be rubbed off.
- The volunteer's name shown in the following ways: made of play dough and placed on to a piece of card; written lightly on paper with a pencil; painted in light-coloured paint on a plastic ice-cream tub lid; drawn on an Etch-a-Sketch; written on a whiteboard in removable pen (not permanent marker).
- A rubber

Talk outline

Ask the congregation if they would consider themselves good at remembering names. Admit that you are either good or bad at remembering names, as appropriate. Point out that people usually like it if someone remembers their name. It can make them feel wanted or cared for. Tell the congregation that you have arranged for someone to help you with the talk today, and ask that person to come to the front without saying their name. Ask if anyone knows what the volunteer is called.

Explain that, because you knew this person was going to help you today, you thought you had better remember what he was called—so you decided to write his name on a few different items.

Show the congregation the card with the name shaped in play dough. Explain that you like play dough and, as you couldn't find a pen at the time, you decided to roll out a long piece and use it to record the volunteer's name. You stuck the name on the card. This seemed like a good idea, but when you picked the card up, the play dough fell off and got messed up, so you ended up rolling it back into a ball again. (Demonstrate the actions as you speak about them.) Now the play dough doesn't remind you of the name at all.

Show the paper with the name pencilled lightly on it. Explain that, next, you thought you'd use a more normal way of recording someone's name, so you wrote it on a piece of paper. However, you had some children playing at your house and one of them found a rubber and rubbed the name out so it could no longer be seen. (Demonstrate as you speak.)

Show the plastic lid with the name painted on it. Explain that you thought you needed to make sure that the name was written in a more permanent way, so you decided to use paint. However, while you were talking to someone, you accidentally scratched off the paint so that the name could no longer be seen. (Demonstrate as you speak.) So even this way was useless at reminding you of the name.

Repeat the demonstration with the Etch-a-Sketch and whiteboard (if available).

Explain that, when none of these reminders worked properly, you had a good idea. Show the congregation the engraving. If it is a plaque that you have had engraved especially for this talk, explain that you decided to get the plaque made. If you are using a piece of jewellery or trophy that the volunteer has lent to you, explain that you borrowed it from them.

If the engraved object is small, ask the children to come forward to look at it. Tell them that, rather than writing the name on an object, you decided it was better to get it engraved. Ask the children why this is a better way to remember something. Point out that the engraving can't be squashed into a ball like the play dough, rubbed out like the pencil, scratched off like the paint, or wiped off like the Etch-a-Sketch or whiteboard. The engraving stays there for ever.

Ask if anyone in the congregation has ever written something on their hand that they needed to remember. Point out that lots of people do this, in the hope that it will jog their memory. Ask the children why it might not be a good idea. Say that, as soon as you wash your hands, the message can disappear, leaving you squinting at the faded letters and

29

desperately trying to work out what they were meant to say.

In the Old Testament, the Israelites were complaining that God had forgotten all about them, and in his reply God said some amazing words. Read Isaiah 49:15–16: 'Can a mother forget the baby at her breast and have no compassion on the child she has borne? Though she may forget, I will not forget you! See, I have engraved you on the palms of my hands.'

Explain that, unfortunately, mothers can sometimes forget about their children, but God will never forget about us. God says he has engraved us on the palms of his hands. Our names will not wash off: they will be there for ever. He will never forget us.

Remind the congregation what an amazing promise this is. No matter what happens to us, even if everyone else eventually forgets about us, God never will.

Challenge

Challenge the congregation to go home and read John 20:24–30, where Jesus appears to Thomas. Ask them to think about how these verses emphasise the truth of today's talk. Ask the children to read them and to tell you next week what the connection is (you may want to offer some incentives). You could have the verses printed on slips of paper for people to take home.

Week 5

LIVING FOR GOD

Aim
To use our bodies to illustrate how we can live for God

Bible links

- Romans 10:15 (Feet)
- Ecclesiastes 9:10 (Hands)
- Matthew 6:22; Hebrews 12:1–2 (Eyes)
- Mark 4:24 (Ears)
- Ephesians 4:29 (Mouth)
- Proverbs 3:5 (Heart)

You will need

- A blank outline of a body drawn on extra large paper (perhaps draw round a member of the congregation beforehand)
- The following parts of the body cut from card: two feet, two hands, two eyes, two ears, mouth and heart

- A box to hold all the items except the heart
- Blu-tack or double-sided sticky tape
- The verses below, displayed on a screen or written on paper for people to read out

How beautiful are the feet of those who bring good news! (Romans 10:15).

Whatever your hand finds to do, do it with all your might (Ecclesiastes 9:10).

The eye is the lamp of the body (Matthew 6:22).

Let us run... fixing our eyes on Jesus (Hebrews 12:1–2).

Consider carefully what you hear (Mark 4:24).

Do not let any unwholesome talk come out of your mouths, but only what is helpful for building others up (Ephesians 4:29).

Trust in the Lord with all your heart and lean not on your own understanding (Proverbs 3:5).

Talk outline

Show the congregation the outline of a person. If you have drawn round somebody present, ask the children to guess who that person is by giving clues (for example, 'This person is male; this person has two children; this person is a fire-fighter', and so on).

Invite a child forward to select an item from the box. Ask them to stick the piece of the body on to the outline in the correct place. If a hand, foot, eye or ear has been selected, ask them to find the other one of the pair and place this on the outline too. The order in which the body parts are chosen doesn't matter, as long as the heart is kept separate to ensure it is the last piece to be placed. You will place it yourself at the end of the talk.

Speak about the importance of each body part as it is placed on the outline.

Feet

Say that feet come in different shapes and sizes. Some people think they have nice feet, while others don't like their feet. (You may or may not want to ask people to put their hands up if they like their feet.) Ask the children what they need feet for. Ask if they knew that the Bible says they can have beautiful feet.

Ask someone to read Romans 10:15: 'How beautiful are the feet of those who bring good news!' Point out that Paul, the writer of the book of Romans, is talking about people travelling around, telling others about Jesus. When the letter was written, people would walk many miles between places because there were no cars, buses or trains. When people walked so far, their feet would be anything but beautiful: they would be dirty and smelly and possibly sore and damaged. However, Paul says that they were beautiful feet because they were walking to give the good news about Jesus.

In the same way today, we can tell the good news about Jesus to other people. We may not be walking as far as Paul and his friends were, but we are still bringing good news and our feet will be beautiful.

Hands

Ask the congregation to look at their hands. Share some interesting facts about hands:

- More men have index fingers shorter than their ring fingers, and more women have index fingers longer than their ring fingers.

- Research shows that top sprinters tend to have long ring fingers.

- Some people can bend their thumbs to their wrists but others will never be able to do so. (Request some demonstrations.)

- There are 27 bones in one hand.

Ask someone to read Ecclesiastes 9:10: 'Whatever your hand finds to do, do it with all your might.'

Ask the children what they think they are good at doing. Point out that most of the things they have said involve using the hands in some way. Remind them that we can use our hands in bad ways. Ask the children for examples (we can steal or hit or use our hands to hurt people in other ways). Say that God has given us hands and he wants us to use them in good ways that will help other people. God doesn't want us to be half-hearted about the things we do. God wants us to work hard and play hard.

Eyes

Ask someone to read Matthew 6:22: 'The eye is the lamp of the body.'

Explain that, for most of us, the information we take in comes mainly through our eyes. This means that what we look at with our eyes is very important. If we look at bad things or watch bad programmes on the television or internet, then we are storing wrong images in our minds. It is often the shocking or unpleasant parts of a TV programme that we remember most clearly. God wants us to let good things enter our minds through our eyes.

Ask someone to read Hebrews 12:1–2: 'Let us run… fixing our eyes on Jesus.'

Ears

Ask someone to read Mark 4:24: 'Consider carefully what you hear.'

Explain that the things we listen to have a great impact on what we think about. If we are listening to unpleasant music all the time, the words in those songs will spring into our minds when we are not expecting it. If we listen to people gossiping and saying unkind things about others, we are much more likely to repeat these things. There are times when we need to walk away from situations where people are being nasty about others. Sometimes we need to make the effort to listen to 'good' things.

Mouth

Ask people to raise their hands if they have heard the saying 'Sticks and stones may break my bones but words will never hurt me.' Point out that, although it is a well-known saying, it is actually incorrect. Words can hurt people badly and their effect can stay with us for a very long time. Once words have been said, they can't ever be unsaid and will stay in people's minds.

Ask someone to read Ephesians 4:29: 'Do not let any unwholesome talk come out of your mouths, but only what is helpful for building others up.'

Explain that we can choose what we do with our mouths. We can use them to hurt people, to be rude and bring others down, or we can use them to say good things, to be kind and to encourage others.

Heart

Say that the heart usually reminds us about love. On Valentine's Day, people send cards with hearts on them to people they love. There are many verses about the heart in the Bible and many verses about how much God loves us.

Ask someone to read Proverbs 3:5: 'Trust in the Lord with all your heart.'

Tell the congregation that we can trust God totally. He knows all about us. He knows our problems and he loves us more than anyone else will ever do. He wants us to use our feet, hands, eyes and ears to help others. As we do this, we can be sure that we can trust God to be with us all the time. Sometimes things happen that we don't understand, but we can trust that God knows what he is doing.

Challenge

Challenge the congregation to try, on at least one occasion in the coming week, to use each part of their bodies in a way that brings them closer to God or helps others.

Week 6

LITTLE THINGS MATTER

Aim
To demonstrate the importance of little things, with special reference to the christening or dedication of a child

Bible links

- Matthew 19:14; Mark 10:14 (Let the children come to me)
- Luke 2:22–40 (Jesus' presentation at the temple)

You will need

- An engagement ring
- A seed or small bulb
- A microchip (or picture of a microchip)

Talk outline

This talk is enhanced if a number of adults are involved. If someone in the congregation has recently become engaged, is an avid gardener or is involved in using technology, ask them beforehand if they would be willing to be interviewed by you during the talk.

If there are a lot of children present, it would be good for them to move to the front, as the things you will be showing them are small. If there is no space to move them to the front, it may be necessary to move round the congregation so that everyone can see what is in your hand.

Hold up the ring, seed and microchip. Ask if anyone has any idea what all three things have in common. The children will probably state that they are all small. Agree with them, but ask them to listen carefully and see if they can work out something else that is special about the three things during the next few minutes.

Ask the person who has recently become engaged to come forward. (If there is no one in the congregation to whom this applies, ask a married person to think back to when they were engaged: the main point is that they are wearing a ring.)

Ask the following questions: 'Could you show us all what you are wearing on your hand? Where did you get the ring from? Who gave it to you? Why is it so important to you?'

Thank the person and, as they return to their seat, comment that it's amazing how something so small can mean such a lot to someone. The ring may be little but it says a massive 'I love you' to the person who receives it.

Hold up the seed and ask a gardener to come to the front. Ask the following questions: 'Why do you like gardening?

Do you know what kind of seed this is? *(Make sure you have told them beforehand, if necessary.)* How can I make this seed grow into a plant? So you mean that this tiny seed can grow into a [name of plant]?'

Thank the person and, as they return to their seat, comment that it is amazing that something so tiny can grow into something so spectacular.

Hold up the microchip and ask the person involved in computing/technology to come to the front. Ask the following questions: 'What is this in my hand? Can you give us some examples of what this little thing can do? How can all that information be stored inside a tiny chip like this?'

Thank the person and, as they return to their seat, comment that it is amazing that something so small can hold so much information and be so powerful.

Hold up each item in turn. Ask the children if they have spotted anything else that all three have in common. Someone should say that they are all small items but they do something big. If the children don't arrive at this answer, ask the wider congregation.

You may want to include the story of a woman called Thérèse who lived over 100 years ago. When Thérèse was four years old, her mother died, leaving her father with five children to look after. Throughout her life Thérèse struggled with illness but she never stopped loving God and she was determined to show that love to other people. Even when she was very poorly she still remained cheerful. Thérèse was not strong enough to do great big things to help people but she discovered that it was often small things that helped others the most. Thérèse became known as 'The little flower' because she would collect flowers and give them out to people who were old or ill. She is famous for her saying, 'What matters in life is not great deeds, but great love', and became known as St Thérèse the Saint of Little Things.

If your service includes the christening or dedication of a baby or child, you could point out that the child may look very small but they are also very important. The Bible tells us about a time when Jesus was very busy. Some parents brought their children to Jesus but his disciples sent them away (Matthew 19:14). However, when Jesus saw what was happening, he stopped the disciples and asked that the children be brought to him so that he could pray for them. He said the famous words, 'Let the little children come to me, and do not hinder them, for the kingdom of heaven belongs to such as these.' Explain that the baby who has been christened or dedicated is very important to God. In the same way, each of us is very important.

Challenge

Ask the children if they can think of any small action that can have a big effect. Examples could be to smile at people, to clear the table after a meal, to say 'thank you', to ask someone who is on their own to join in a game, and so on. Challenge the congregation to think of two things they could do this week that may seem little but could have a big effect on someone. You may like to see if someone will share their experience next week.

Week 7

PASS ON THE LOVE

Aim
To show that, if we all pass God's love on to people, it will multiply very quickly

Bible links

- John 3:16 (God loved the world)
- 1 John 3:1; Romans 5:8 (God's great love)
- 1 John 4:7–10; John 13:34–35 (Sharing God's love with others)

You will need

- Hundreds of small red heart stickers
- A large red heart shape cut from card

If this talk is being used close to Valentine's Day, it's helpful to have a collection of cards showing a red heart, with short verses, poems or statements saying 'I love you'.

Talk outline

Show the children the large red heart shape. Ask them when they would expect to see a heart like this and what it usually means. Show the selection of Valentine's cards, if available. Ask the children to read out some of the verses. Ask what these Valentine's Day cards are trying to tell the person reading the card. The answer is 'I love you!'

Say that a Valentine's Day card is a good way to express love for someone but there are many other ways, too. Ask if the children can think of any other ways that we might show someone that we love them.

Point out that the Bible tells us that God loves us very much. Ask three prearranged volunteers to read the following verses:

For God so loved the world that he gave his one and only Son, that whoever believes in him shall not perish but have eternal life (John 3:16).

See what great love the Father has lavished on us, that we should be called children of God! And that is what we are! (1 John 3:1).

But God demonstrates his own love for us in this: while we were still sinners, Christ died for us (Romans 5:8).

Explain that God showed his love for us when he sent Jesus. Read 1 John 4:9: 'This is how God showed his love among us: he sent his one and only Son into the world that we might live through him.'

Then say that although the Bible speaks a lot about God's love for us, it has something else very important to say about love. Read John 13:34–35: 'A new command I give you: love one another. As I have loved you, so you must love one another. By this everyone will know that you are my disciples, if you love one another.'

Explain that God wants us to pass his love on to each other. He wants us to share his love with people who don't yet know about it.

Show the children one of the small heart stickers. Ask for a volunteer to come to the front and invite them to stick one sticker on to their clothes. Now ask them to take another sticker and give it to someone in the congregation, asking them to stick it on to their clothes. Now ask the two people wearing stickers to collect another sticker each and give them to two other people. Ask these four people to collect a sticker and give it to four others. Continue to do this for as long as you feel it is appropriate. The numbers start small but suddenly expand as each person passes on a heart: 1, 2, 4, 8, 16, 32, 64, 128, 256 and so on.

Make the point that all this heart-giving started with just one person. Explain that the hearts are meant to represent God's love. If we are willing to pass God's love on to just one person at a time, it can quickly make a massive difference.

This talk works well if the heart-giving continues until everyone in the congregation has been given a heart. Emphasise that now the church is so full of God's love that it will have to overflow to the people outside whom we meet every day.

Remind the congregation that God loved us so much that he sent Jesus into the world to die on the cross, so that we could be forgiven and be friends with God. Once we are friends with God and have realised how much he loves us, then we will want to pass his love on to others.

Challenge

Challenge the congregation to pass God's love on to one person this week. Encourage them to look for opportunities to show this love as well as to speak about it.

Week 8

SPREADING THE NEWS

Aim
To show that everyone has a part to play in spreading the good news about Jesus

Bible links

- Matthew 4:18–20; Mark 1:16–18 (Jesus calls the first disciples)
- Luke 10:1–2 (Jesus sends out the 72)
- Matthew 28:18–20 (The great commission)

You will need

- Lots of small pictures of people or lots of smiley faces
- Two empty containers
- Chairs
- A simple sail
- Pretend fishing rods (optional). You could place magnets on the end of the rods and make paper fish, with paperclips attached, to be caught.

Talk outline

Before the service begins, scatter the small pictures of people or smiley faces over the floor, all around the room. Make sure they are scattered far enough away from the front to make the task more difficult. There need to be enough for the children present to be able to collect three or four each.

Also in advance, set up the chairs in a boat shape, with the seats facing inwards. Alternatively, ask the children to watch carefully as you position the chairs, putting their hands up when they can guess what you are making. Ask for volunteers to come and sit in the boat and, if a sail is available, ask two of the volunteers to hold it. If you are using paper fish, scatter them around the boat.

Remind the congregation that at least four of Jesus' disciples were fishermen and much of Jesus' ministry was centred on the Sea of Galilee. Ask the volunteers to pretend to fish over the side of the boat. If 'fishing rods' are available, ask the volunteers to hold them.

Tell the story of Jesus calling the first disciples to follow him, as found in Matthew 4:18–20 and Mark 1:16–18. Explain that Jesus first saw Andrew and Peter in their boat and a little later he saw James and John. These fishermen were used to being out on the lake catching fish, but Jesus said that he would help them to 'fish for people'. Ask if anyone knows what Jesus meant by this. Explain that Jesus wanted these fishermen first of all to follow him and then to go out to tell other people about him. As people listened to Andrew, Peter, James and John, they would follow Jesus.

Ask for four volunteers. Show them the pictures of people or smiley faces scattered around the room and tell them to collect as many of the pictures as they can and place them in one of the empty containers, while the congregation counts down from ten. You may wish the volunteers to collect one picture and place it in the container before they collect a second. Say, 'On your marks... get set... go!' and lead the congregation in the countdown. As soon as you reach zero, stop the volunteers.

Now ask for more volunteers. You may want to invite all the children to join in or just add eight more to the original four, to represent the twelve disciples. Tell them to collect as many pictures as they can and place them in the other empty container, while the congregation counts down from ten again. Say, 'On your marks... get set... go!' and lead the congregation in another countdown. As soon as you reach zero, stop the volunteers.

Show the congregation the two containers. Point out that in the first container there are far fewer pictures. Explain that Jesus first called four disciples to fish for people. Then he called more people until he had twelve disciples. After that, he sent 72 people out to tell others about him—to fish for people (Luke 10:1–2). Jesus wanted more and more people to follow him, so he needed to send out more fishermen.

Explain that before he went back to heaven, Jesus gave the 'great commission', saying that his followers should tell everyone in the world about him. Read Matthew 28:18–20: 'Then Jesus came to them and said, "... Therefore go and make disciples of all nations, baptising them in the name of the Father and of the Son and of the Holy Spirit, and teaching them to obey everything I have commanded you. And surely I am with you always, to the very end of the age."'

Remind the congregation of how many more pictures of people or faces were gathered up by the larger group of volunteers. The more people who go out and tell others about Jesus, the quicker the news about Jesus will spread and the more people will follow him.

Challenge

Challenge the congregation to begin to pray for someone this week, with whom they would like to share the love of Jesus. Challenge them to pray for an opportunity to invite them to church or to speak to them about following Jesus. In this way they too can fish for people.

Week 9

SPOT THE DIFFERENCE

Aim

To demonstrate that there should be some differences in the lives of Christians that are noticeable to other people

---

Bible links

- Philippians 2:14–15 (Shining stars)
- Matthew 5:13–16; Mark 9:50 (Salt and light)
- Romans 12:2 (Don't conform)
- John 17:15–16 (Being protected in the world)
- 1 Peter 2:9–12 (Living good lives)

You will need

- A bottle of diet Coke and a bottle of standard Coke, or a bottle of Pepsi and a bottle of Coke
- A type of biscuit (for example, digestives or custard creams) in an expensive brand and a similar-looking equivalent in a cheaper brand

- A bar of well-known chocolate and a similar-looking bar of cheap chocolate
- A table and cloth
- Blindfolds
- Two cups for each person taking the test, labelled so that only you know which contains each type of cola

Talk outline

Place the cola, biscuits and chocolate on the table and cover them with the cloth.

Explain that you are going to need some volunteers who are willing to taste things while blindfolded. If possible, ask young people or adults to volunteer, as they tend to be more entertaining. If children are to take part, make sure that their parents are present or check with the children's leaders that they have no allergies.

Show the congregation the two bottles of Coke (or Coke and Pepsi) and ask who prefers one or the other. Ask if anyone really thinks they can tell the difference between the two and ask one of these people to come to the front to take the ultimate test.

Blindfold the volunteer and ask the congregation to keep quiet. Pour a different cola into each cup, making it clear to the congregation which cup contains which. Place one cup in the volunteer's hand and ask them to have a drink. Repeat with the other cup. Ask the volunteer to guess which cola is which. Remove the blindfold and tell the volunteer whether or not they were correct. You may want to allow other people to have a go, or leave the cola and extra cups for people to try after the service.

Ask for a volunteer who likes biscuits. Tell them that you have two different brands of the same kind of biscuit and you want to see if they can distinguish between them. Blindfold the volunteer, ask them to test the biscuits and tell them whether or not they guessed correctly. Repeat this process with the two brands of chocolate.

Hold up the chocolate, and then the biscuits, showing that there is very little difference between them, to look at. Point out that until we eat them, we can have no idea which will taste better.

Hold the cups of cola next to each other and say, again, that we can't see any difference between them. It is only when we drink them that we may be able to taste a difference, and even then, many people can't tell the difference at all.

Read Matthew 5:13–16. In this passage Jesus talks about Christians as salt and light. Ask the children what salt is used for. Explain that salt can be used as a preservative and that it also brings out the flavour in food, making it taste better. Jesus is saying that, if you simply look at food, you cannot see whether or not it contains salt. However, when the food is eaten, the presence of salt will be obvious: the food will have lots of flavour and will not have gone off. In the same way, Christians look exactly the same as everyone else in the world, but the effect we have should mean that people can spot the difference.

Read Philippians 2:14–15: 'Do everything without grumbling or arguing, so that you may become blameless and pure, "children of God without fault in a warped and crooked generation". Then you will shine among them like stars in the sky.'

Emphasise the phrase 'you shine among them like stars in the sky'. Ask people to think about the places where they spend time during the week. Do they shine like stars in the night sky that can't be missed, or does no one notice that they are different?

Point out that Paul, the writer of Philippians, focuses on something very interesting that he says will show that we are different. Re-read the start of verse 14: 'Do everything without grumbling or arguing…'. Sometimes little things can make a huge difference.

Challenge

Ask the congregation to look back over the last week and remember any times when they have grumbled and argued. Ask them to imagine what a difference it would make in school, in the home or in the workplace if they never argued and never grumbled. Challenge them to try not to complain about anything for one week. Encourage them to tell someone else that they are going to try to do this, in case they need reminding.

Week 10

FIX YOUR EYES

Aim
To demonstrate that when we focus on Jesus, other things don't matter so much. This could be tied in with the theme of Lent

Bible links

- Hebrews 12:2; 2 Corinthians 4:18 (Fix your eyes)
- Hebrews 3:1 (Fix your thoughts on Jesus)
- Deuteronomy 11:18 (Fix God's words in your hearts)

You will need

- A plastic cup and a jug of water
- A prize for the volunteer
- A large picture showing lots of money; a picture of a large detached house; two pictures of famous people; a picture of a desirable car

Talk outline

Arrange for five adults to be positioned at different places among the congregation, each holding one of the pictures. Another adult is needed at the back of the room, with a jug of water.

Ask for a volunteer who has very steady hands and won't get too nervous if everyone is watching them. This volunteer will be carrying water, so it is very important that they can concentrate and move slowly. An older child or young person is preferable to a young child.

Give the volunteer an empty plastic cup and ask them to practise walking while carrying the cup steadily. When they have practised a few times, move them to the back of the room and ask the adult to fill the cup to the brim with water. The cup must be as full as possible so that the volunteer has to concentrate hard.

Encourage the water carrier to move as carefully as possible to the front of the room. (If the room is small, leave a space round the outside so that the carrier can move round that track.) Point out that there is no prize for completing the task quickly. The only prize is for arriving at the front without spilling one drop.

As the carrier begins to walk forward, the person in the congregation who is holding the picture of the money should quietly stand up and lift it in the air. A moment later, the person with the picture of the house should do likewise. As this person stands, the money holder should sit down. This should be repeated with the pictures of the two famous people, and the water carrier should be so focused on the task in hand that they should not see the people stand up, but other members of the congregation should see them clearly.

Make sure that all the picture holders are seated before the volunteer arrives at the front of the room. Take the cup from the volunteer and congratulate them on their steady hands. Now ask them if they can tell you what they saw on their way to the front. Explain that various people held up pictures for them to see. Ask the people in the congregation to stand and hold up the pictures again.

Say that the volunteer was so focused on the cup of water that they didn't see any of the distractions appearing around them (or so distracted that they spilt the water). Tell the congregation that the Bible has something very important to say about this.

Read Hebrews 12:1–2: 'Let us throw off everything that hinders and the sin that so easily entangles. And let us run with perseverance the race marked out for us, fixing our eyes on Jesus, the pioneer and perfecter of faith.'

Explain that, as we go through our lives, it is important to keep our eyes fixed on Jesus. Mention each of the pictures that the people are holding and say that it's not wrong to have any of these things. Often, however, the desire for more money, a big house, an expensive car, fame or popularity can distract us from following Jesus. We need to keep our eyes fixed on him.

Read Hebrews 3:1: 'Therefore, holy brothers and sisters… fix your thoughts on Jesus.'

One of the best ways to make sure we keep our eyes

on Jesus is to spend time thinking about him. We can do this by reading the Bible (Deuteronomy 11:18), going to church, listening to Christian music, and so on. As we fix our thoughts and eyes on Jesus, the other things around us become less important.

If this service is linked to the season of Lent, make the point that, as Christians approach Easter, they spend time focusing their eyes on Jesus in a special way. They want to be ready for the celebration of his death and resurrection, so they spend extra time thinking about God. Many people give something up during Lent—for example, watching less television or not eating a certain type of food. Other people do something positive during the Lent season, such as taking on an extra chore around the house or doing something kind for someone every day. Lent lasts for 40 days—a reminder of the length of time that Jesus spent fasting in the wilderness.

Challenge

Explain that the things we read, watch and listen to, and even the friends that we spend time with, can affect the way we think. Encourage the congregation to think about whether the things they put into their minds are helpful in focusing their thoughts on Jesus. Challenge them to switch off the television at some point in the coming week and spend time reading part of the Bible instead.

If this talk is used during the season of Lent, challenge the congregation to make a commitment to something positive over the next 40 days.

Week 11

SINCE WE WERE BABIES

<table>
<tr><td>

Aim

To illustrate that God has been with us from the moment of conception and that he will always remain with us. To use the idea of milk and solid food to show that we need to continue to 'grow up' as Christians

</td></tr>
</table>

Bible links

- Psalm 139:13–16 (God knew us before we were born)
- 1 Corinthians 3:2; Hebrews 5:12 (Milk or solid food)

You will need

- Pictures of members of the congregation as babies (to be displayed digitally, or enlarged to be clearly visible)
- A collection of baby clothes, including shoes
- A bottle of milk, some baby food and some solid food (for example, pizza or cake)

Talk outline

Ask the congregation to think back in time as far as they can remember. What is their earliest memory? Ask a few people to share their memories. You may wish to prearrange this with someone who has a special memory from early in their lives.

Explain that a number of photographs are going to appear on the screen and you want people to guess who the pictures show. Display the photographs one at a time and allow a few guesses from the congregation. If, after a few guesses, the baby has still not been identified, invite three or four people to the front, one of whom is the person in the photograph. See if people can now distinguish which person is the baby in the photograph. Repeat until all the babies are identified.

Point out to the children that one thing everybody in the room has in common is that they were all once babies. Sometimes that's hard to imagine when we see adults, but even the oldest person was once a baby; at some point everybody has been born. (If you have a young baby in the congregation, it would be good to introduce them to the rest of the congregation.)

Ask a selection of children to come to the front. Show everyone the baby shoes. Casually give them to one of the older children and ask them to put them on. Show another item of babywear and ask another child to put that on. Continue doing this as the children look confused. Point out that every one of these children would, at one time, have fitted into these clothes, but now that they have grown bigger they can't do it any more.

Explain that, in the same way as babies grow into children and then into adults, God wants us to grow up as Christians. When we are very little, it is brilliant to learn Bible stories such as Noah's ark, the feeding of the 5000, and Daniel in the lions' den. As we get older, it is important to look a bit more carefully at the Bible and listen to the stories but also apply what they say to our lives.

Show the baby's bottle and ask the children who would drink from it. Show the baby food and ask who would eat it. Show the pizza or cake and ask who would eat it: the children will probably react hungrily. Say that, as children and adults, we wouldn't want to drink from a bottle or eat baby food: we would rather eat the solid food.

Read Hebrews 5:12: 'In fact, though by this time you ought to be teachers... you need milk, not solid food!'

Reiterate that, as we get older, God doesn't want us just to listen to Bible stories; he wants us to think about them and try to understand what they are teaching us. He wants us then to go and do what they say.

Challenge

Challenge the children to read a Bible story each day this week and take time to think about what the story can teach them. Challenge the rest of the congregation to do the same with a Bible passage.

Week 12

HANDS THAT TALK

Aim

To demonstrate that we can use our hands in
ways that point people towards Jesus.
This talk could be used as part of a
Mother's Day service

Bible links

- Mark 10:13–16 (Children come to Jesus)
- Matthew 8:1–4 (People with leprosy)
- Luke 13:10–13 (A crippled woman)
- Mark 1:30–31 (A woman with a fever)

You will need

- A large hand cut out of card
- Pieces of paper with actions written on (see below)
- Galatians 6:10 printed out, large enough to be
  displayed
- Someone who can teach a few statements using sign
  language (optional)

Talk outline

Ask the children to come to the front, explaining that you need them to listen very carefully to something. Produce the large hand and put it to your ear, pretending that you are straining to hear something. Put your finger to your lips and ask everyone to be as quiet as possible. Ask the children if they can hear anything. When the children say they can't hear anything, hold the large hand against a few of their ears and ask if they can hear anything then. Explain that, even though this large card hand doesn't seem to speak, actually our hands can speak very loudly.

Ask for volunteers who would like to do some simple acting to come forward one at a time. (If you are involving younger children, who will need the instructions read quietly to them, you may like to have another adult at the front ready to do this—or make sure your microphone is switched off.) Explain that the volunteers are going to carry out a simple action and you want the rest of the congregation to guess what they are trying to say.

Show each volunteer one of the instructions written on paper:

- Saying 'goodbye': wave
- Asking for quiet: finger to lips
- Telling someone off: wag finger
- Being angry: shake fist
- Showing care: put arm round someone, or hold hands
- Saying 'well done' at a show: clapping

- Saying 'well done' generally: thumbs up
- Having scored a goal (or other success): high 5

Once all the actions have been guessed, point out that none of the volunteers spoke words. Their hands spoke for them.

If possible, ask someone to teach the congregation a few phrases or a song using sign language. Explain that, when someone is deaf, they use their hands to speak all the time.

Say that in the Bible Jesus often used his hands to speak. Read Mark 10:13–16 or retell the story. Point out that when the disciples were sending the children away, Jesus stopped them, took time to be with the children and put his hands on them to pray for them. This showed everybody how important he thought the children were.

Read or retell the story of the men with leprosy in Matthew 8:1–4, putting particular emphasis on verse 3, where Jesus reaches out his hand to touch the men. Explain that leprosy was a feared disease in biblical times but Jesus still touched people who had the disease: he truly cared about them.

Read or retell the story in Luke 13:10–13, emphasising verse 13, where Jesus places his hands on the woman and she is healed.

Mention that there are many other stories in which Jesus reaches out to touch people. Often, these people were unpopular or considered unworthy or unclean by the religious leaders of the time. However, Jesus wanted to make it clear that, in his eyes, everyone mattered. Jesus used his hands to speak of his love and care to those in need. He also used his hands to show people who disapproved of his actions that there was another way to live, a way that encouraged and cared for people rather than criticising and marginalising them.

Explain that our hands can speak today. We can use our hands to push people away or to show people we care.

Display Galatians 6:10 and ask the congregation to read it together: 'Therefore, as we have opportunity, let us do good to all people.'

Challenge

Challenge the congregation to seek to use their hands to show love to at least one person every day this week.

Challenge them not to take the easy option but to actively seek to show this care to someone they find more difficult to love, or to someone whom others tend to avoid.

Week 13

GETTING RID

Aim
To illustrate that Jesus' death on the cross was to get rid of all the wrong things that we do

Bible links

- 1 John 3:5; Colossians 2:14 (He took away our sin)
- John 19:16–30 (Crucifixion)

You will need

- A selection of small items that are used for 'getting rid' of something, stored in a bag (for example: duster, washing-up liquid, toothbrush, toy pick-up truck, car cleaning equipment, flannel, soap)
- Vacuum cleaner, bin and lawn mower (optional)
- Pictures displayed on screen showing people carrying out jobs that 'get rid' of something (for example: a fire-fighter putting out a fire; a dentist drilling away decay; a rubbish collector emptying the bins; a street cleaning vehicle)

Talk outline

You may wish to ask the children to move to the front so that they can see the objects you have brought more clearly. Show the congregation each item in turn. Ask the children the name of each object and explain what it would be used for. You may like to ask a volunteer to act out the item's use as you produce it from your bag. Try to make this funny by asking people who might not usually be expected to wash up or do the cleaning.

If available, show the pictures of people carrying out their jobs. Ask the children to name the jobs and to explain what is happening in the pictures.

Quickly name each object and job in turn and ask if anyone can guess what they all have in common. Initially the children will probably say 'cleaning', so point out the tractor, lawn mower and fire-fighter.

If necessary, give clues until someone realises that all of the objects seen, and all of the jobs shown, get rid of something. A duster gets rid of cobwebs and dust, a pick-up truck gets rid of broken-down cars, a fire-fighter gets rid of fire, and so on.

Explain that the Bible talks about getting rid of things. Ephesians 4:31, Colossians 3:8 and 1 Peter 2:1 all talk about getting rid of bad things from our lives. (See also Week 52, 'Throw it away'.) However, today you want to think about something else that the Bible speaks about getting rid of. Ask the children if they have any idea what it could be.

Ask the congregation to listen carefully while you read two verses. Explain that the words 'get rid of' don't actually appear in them, but very similar words do. Ask the children to spot what is 'got rid of' in each verse.

Read 1 John 3:5: 'Jesus appeared so that he might take away our sins.'

Read Colossians 2:13–14: 'He forgave us all our sin... he has taken it away, nailing it to the cross.'

When the children spot that it is our sin that has been taken away, ask them what 'sin' is. Explain that, in the Bible, sin refers to anything that puts up a barrier between us and God. It could be things we do that are wrong or it could be things we don't do that we should do, such as loving and caring for other people.

Explain that Jesus died so that we could be forgiven for all the things that cause this barrier between us and God. Romans 5:8 says, 'God demonstrates his own love for us in this: while we were still sinners, Christ died for us.' Jesus was punished instead of us for the wrong things that we have done. As it says in Colossians 2:14, our sins were nailed to the cross. If we ask God to forgive us, then all our sin can be got rid of and we can be God's friend.

Repeat both Bible verses, using the words 'got rid of' instead to emphasise the point: 'Jesus appeared so that he might get rid of our sins' (1 John 3:5) and 'He forgave us all our sin... he got rid of it, nailing it to the cross' (Colossians 2:13–14).

Challenge

Challenge the children to make a list of objects or jobs that get rid of something. You may want to offer to give prizes next week for those with the longest lists.

Challenge the whole congregation to think about these two verses as they clean things or throw things out this week. Ask them to thank God that our sins are forgiven, every time they put something in the bin.

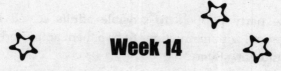

Week 14

CELEBRATE

Aim
To use different celebrations to point people towards the meaning of Palm Sunday

Bible links

- Mark 11:1–11 (Entry into Jerusalem)

You will need

- Birthday banner; birthday cake with candles
- Party poppers; recording of 'Auld Lang Syne' (optional)
- Confetti; top hat and veil (optional)
- Flags
- Branches or palm leaves made out of sticks and paper; coats
- The words 'Hosanna! Blessed is he who comes in the name of the Lord!' printed out large enough for the congregation to read
- A song about Palm Sunday or one including the word 'Hosanna'

Give the party poppers to sensible adults seated in the congregation, with instructions to pop them at the end of the song 'Auld Lang Syne'.

Talk outline

Ask the children if they have ever been to a celebration. Explain that you need some volunteers to show the kinds of things that happen at some well-known celebrations.

Ask if anyone in the congregation has a birthday this week. If they do, invite them to the front. Invite two volunteers to hold the birthday banner. Bring out the birthday cake, light the candles and ask the congregation to sing.

Ask for volunteers who have been to a New Year's Eve celebration. Invite them to cross their arms and link hands as the congregation joins in singing 'Auld Lang Syne'. (To help people to join in, download the song ready to play or prearrange for someone to sing it.) As the song ends, adults in the congregation should pop the party poppers they have been given.

Ask for two volunteers to pretend to get married. Dress them up, if you wish. As they stand side by side, ask a few volunteers to throw confetti over them.

Ask the children if they have ever seen anyone famous. Has anyone lined up on the streets to see someone famous walk or drive past? Has anyone ever seen a member of the royal family? Explain that when a member of the royal family arrives somewhere, people in the crowd will often cheer and wave flags or banners. Invite a few children to come to the front and hold a flag. Invite someone to pretend to be famous and walk past the children as they cheer and wave their flags, or ask the children to cheer on the count of three.

Encourage the children to imagine what they could do if they had arrived at a birthday party to find that everyone had forgotten about the cake. Ask them what they could do if they were at a wedding and the bride and groom were desperate to have a photograph with confetti being thrown, but nobody had brought any. What could they do if they were waiting for the royal family to arrive and realised that nobody had any flags?

Explain that, in the Bible, the Jewish people often went to Jerusalem for special celebrations. The greatest of these celebrations was the Passover, when people remembered how God had once rescued the Jews from slavery in Egypt. Whole families would often travel to Jerusalem to celebrate, and Jesus did this with his family when he was younger (see Luke 2:41–52).

Tell how, in each of the four Gospels, we read about the time just before Jesus died when he went into Jerusalem with his disciples. Only a short time before this, Jesus had carried out an amazing miracle by raising his friend Lazarus from the dead. Many people had heard about it and were wondering if Jesus would come to Jerusalem for the Passover. They wondered what they would see Jesus do, and many of them thought he was so important and powerful that he would overthrow the Romans who ruled in that area at the time.

Many years before, God had made a promise to send a special king called the 'Messiah', who would be the ruler of the Jews. The Jewish people had been waiting a long time for that king to arrive. Some of them thought that Jesus could be the promised Messiah. When the crowd heard that Jesus and his disciples were on their way, they lined the streets to cheer him. They took palm branches off the trees so that they had something to wave and even took their coats off so that they could lay them on the ground for Jesus to walk on. Jesus came into Jerusalem riding on a donkey—the only time recorded in the Bible when Jesus rode on an animal. There was a feeling of great celebration.

Give out the paper palm branches for children to hold. Tell them that the crowd shouted, 'Hosanna! Blessed is he who comes in the name of the Lord!' The people wanted to praise God.

Explain that the congregation is going to stand as they sing a song. As they sing, you want the children to walk up and down waving their branches and shouting 'Hosanna!' They can also lay coats on the ground, like the crowds did for Jesus and his donkey.

Challenge

Challenge the children to take their paper palm branches home and place them in their bedrooms. Ask them to look at the branches each day in the coming week and say a 'thank you' prayer to God for something he has done for them.

The people in the crowd, on the day Jesus entered Jerusalem, would all have had different thoughts about him. Some of them would have thought he was a good man, some a prophet, some the Messiah, some a fraud. As we move towards Easter, challenge the congregation to think about who they believe Jesus really is.

FESTIVE FOOD

Aim
To remind people of the Easter story through a range of foods that are available at Easter

Bible links

A variety of Easter passages or passages referring to the Passover could be used.

- Luke 22:1–6, 47–48 (Judas' decision)
- John 13:18–30 (Last supper)
- Matthew 27:32–50; Mark 15:21–42; Luke 23:26–49; John 19:16–42 (Crucifixion)
- Matthew 28:1–10; Mark 16:1–8; Luke 24:1–12; John 20:1–18 (Resurrection)
- Exodus 12:1–3 (Passover)

You will need

- A picture of a roast lamb dinner
- A traditional simnel cake with eleven marzipan balls on top

- Hot cross buns
- A hollow Easter egg

Talk outline

Ask people to tell you about their favourite foods. If they were allowed to choose a special meal for their birthday, what meal would it be? Seasons of the year sometimes have special food associated with them. Ask what food you might eat in the summer (barbecues, ice cream) and at Christmas (turkey, sprouts) and ask if anyone can think of a food particularly associated with Easter. The answer will probably be Easter eggs. Explain that you are going to show them four foods that are traditionally eaten during the Easter season, which all have special meanings that point towards the Easter story.

Show the children the picture of the roast lamb. Just as turkey is the traditional Christmas food, so lamb is the traditional Easter roast. Ask if anyone knows why this is the case. Explain that a long time before Jesus was born, God rescued the people of Israel from slavery in Egypt. (You may want to remind the children quickly about Moses, the plagues, fleeing from Egypt, and crossing the Red Sea.) On the night when the Israelites left Egypt, God gave them some instructions to protect them from the final plague (the death of the firstborn Egyptians). First, they had to mark the doorposts of their homes with blood from a lamb that had been killed, so that when God 'passed over' their houses they would be spared from the effects of this last plague. The families were instructed then to get dressed ready for a long journey, roast the lamb, eat it with herbs and unleavened bread, and then leave quickly.

Over the years, the Israelites continued to remember this last meal before their escape from Egypt, and the festival became known as Passover. In Jesus' time, many people would travel to Jerusalem to celebrate Passover. The Easter story in the Bible takes place during the Passover celebration, and Jesus is sometimes called the 'Lamb of God'.

Show the children the simnel cake and ask if they can think what it has to do with the Easter story. After taking a few guesses, ask the children to count the number of marzipan balls. Why are there eleven of them? Say that you are going to give them a clue, and (even if they have already guessed the answer) read Mark 14:17: 'When evening came, Jesus arrived with the twelve.' Ask who the twelve other people were and, when the answer 'the disciples' is given, point out that the marzipan balls represent the disciples. So why are there only eleven? Explain that Judas betrayed Jesus and handed him over to the soldiers, so he is not included on the cake.

Show the children the hot cross buns and ask how these could tie in with the Easter story. Someone will guess that the cross on the top reminds us of Jesus and his death. Ask why it is important to remember this. Explain that Jesus died so that we could be forgiven for all the wrong things we have done.

Show the children the Easter eggs and ask what they have to do with Easter. Say that they remind us of two things. First, they remind us that Jesus was placed in a tomb with a huge stone rolled in front of it: the egg represents the stone. (This idea could be tied in with the traditional egg-rolling that takes place in some regions, which is symbolic of the stone being rolled away from Jesus' tomb.) Second, and more importantly, they remind us (break open the egg) that the tomb of Jesus was empty when people went to look on the morning of Easter Day, because Jesus was no longer dead. He was alive again.

In the traditional Easter foods we have the whole Easter story. Jesus was in Jerusalem for the Passover. He was there with his disciples but Judas betrayed him and handed him over to the soldiers. Jesus was crucified. He was placed in a tomb and a huge stone was rolled in front of it. Jesus rose from the dead and is now alive for ever.

Ask the children what can hatch out of a real egg. Say that a chick hatching out of an egg is symbolic of new life. We can have a new life with Jesus because of what he has done for us.

Challenge

During the next few days or weeks, there are going to be many Easter foods displayed in the shops and many Easter eggs waiting to be eaten in people's homes. Challenge the whole congregation that when they see any of these foods they should say 'thank you' to God for the wonderful truth of the Easter story.

Week 16

THE GOOD SHEPHERD

Aim

To help explain why Jesus would describe himself as the good shepherd

Bible links

* John 10:11–15 (The good shepherd)

You will need

* Chairs set up in a square shape, with one chair missing to make a doorway
* A cloak, headdress and staff
* Volunteers to act as a wild bear or wolf (if possible, with a mask) and a robber

Talk outline

Set out the chairs before the talk begins.

Dress up as a shepherd with the cloak, headdress and staff, and ask the children to guess what your new occupation is. Once they have guessed, ask what they think a shepherd does as part of his job. In New Testament times, shepherds were usually very poor and were not highly respected. Despite this, Jesus often compared himself to a shepherd.

During the day, shepherds would take their flocks out into the fields to find fresh grass. In the evening, they would place the sheep into a fold to keep them safe from wild animals. If the shepherds were grazing the sheep close to their home town, they would take the sheep to a fold made of stones. If they were grazing in pastures a long way from home, the shepherds would build a makeshift fold from branches and thorns.

Show the congregation the sheepfold you have made out of chairs, and explain that the sheep would enter by the gap. Ask for volunteers to play sheep. As the children come to the front, herd them into the fold, speaking to them as their shepherd: 'Here, sheepy, sheepy. In you go, nice and safe from those nasty wild animals. I'm not having any wolf or bear attacking my favourite sheep...'

Once the sheep are in the fold, explain to the rest of the congregation that, in biblical times, the shepherd would sleep at the entrance to the fold to make sure that no wild animal or sheep stealer could enter there. If there was a gate at the entrance, the shepherd would lie in front of it. More often, though, there would simply be a gap and the shepherd himself would be the 'gate' or the 'door'.

Say that while you go to sleep, it would be helpful if the congregation could keep watch and shout to you if anyone comes to attack. Say 'goodnight' to the sheep, lie down in the doorway and pretend to go to sleep.

This part of the talk can be made as long or short as is appropriate for the congregation. The volunteer dressed as a wild animal should tiptoe towards the fold, looking round menacingly. Hopefully, the children and adults will shout to you to wake up. You may want to look round as the wild animal 'hides', and then fall back to sleep again. Repeat as often as appropriate. Eventually you can spot the animal, jump up, and scare it away.

Lie down and pretend to go back to sleep. A moment later, the volunteer dressed as a robber should arrive and try to climb over the chairs. Again, the congregation should shout to wake you up. Jump up and scare the robber away.

Explain that, sometimes, sheepfolds were built large enough to hold several different flocks. If this was the case, a watchman might be hired to cover the doorway while the shepherds went to sleep. Each shepherd would then get up in the morning, stand at the entrance to the fold and call out to the sheep. Those belonging to each flock would recognise their own shepherd's voice and would walk out of the fold. The sheep that did not recognise the shepherd's voice would stay inside until called by their own shepherd.

Read John 10:11–15 and pick out the main points:

- We are the sheep.
- Jesus says he is the gate for the sheep. If we put our trust in him, we are safe. He will protect us and give us 'life in all its fullness'.
- Jesus describes himself as the good shepherd. If someone was hired to look after the sheep, then they

might run away when trouble or danger arrived. However, Jesus loves us so much that he would give up his life for us—and did so on the cross.

- Jesus says that his followers will recognise his voice and follow him, knowing that they are safe with him.

Challenge

Read part of John 10:4 again: 'His sheep follow him because they know his voice.' Challenge the congregation to ask themselves whether they know Jesus' voice. Encourage them to read John 10 this week and to think about what the passage means to them.

Week 17

KEEPING HEALTHY

Aim
To use the idea of keeping our bodies fit to consider how we can keep spiritually fit

Bible links

- Hebrews 10:25 (Meet together)
- 1 Thessalonians 5:17 (Pray continually)
- Psalm 119:105 (God's word is a lamp)
- 1 Corinthians 10:31 (Do things for God's glory)
- Psalm 46:10 (Be still)
- Psalm 62:5 (Find rest)

You will need

- Dumbbells or other fitness equipment
- A pillow or duvet
- Some food (vegetables, loaf of bread, and so on)
- The words 'exercise', 'sleep' and 'healthy diet' written on cards or displayed on the screen

Talk outline

Ask the children if any of them have ever been ill. Ask if they can think of anything that could stop them from becoming ill and could keep them fit and healthy. Allow the children to answer before opening up the question to the wider congregation.

Explain that there are four main things we can do to keep healthy. The first is to keep away from things that can harm us. It is silly to do dangerous things or to put yourself into situations where you could be injured or become sick. However, today you want to think about three positive things that people can do to stay healthy. Explain that you have three things written on cards and you want the children to guess what each card says.

Show the different foods and ask the children what they think the first card is going to say. Ask a child to hold up the 'healthy diet' card. If we want our bodies to work properly, we need to eat a good balanced diet. If we were to eat nothing but sweets, we would become ill; if we ate nothing but vegetables, we would also become ill. We need to put food into our bodies that will help us stay fit and healthy.

Show the dumbbells or fitness equipment and ask the children what they think the second card will say. Ask a child to hold up the 'exercise' card. All of us need to exercise if our bodies are to be fit and healthy.

Show the pillow or duvet and ask the children what they think the third card will say. Ask a child to hold up the 'sleep' card. Even if we eat well and exercise a lot, we will still become ill if we don't have enough sleep.

Explain that just as we need to have a healthy diet, exercise and sleep to keep us healthy physically, we need similar things to keep us healthy spiritually. When we become a Christian, we need to do certain things if we are to grow in our relationship with God.

The 'healthy diet' reminds us that it is important to put good things into our lives if we are to grow in our relationship with God. We need to spend time with other Christians (Hebrews 10:25: 'Do not give up meeting together, as some are in the habit of doing, but let us encourage each other'); we need to pray (1 Thessalonians 5:17: 'Pray continually'); we need to spend time reading our Bibles (Psalm 119:105). If we do these things, they will help to keep our relationship with God healthy.

The 'exercise' card reminds us that if we are to grow as Christians, we need to carry out some actions. James 2:17 says that if we simply believe in God but don't do any good deeds, it is just like having no belief in him at all ('Faith by itself, if it is not accompanied by action, is dead'). 1 Corinthians 10:31 tells us, 'So whether you eat or drink or whatever you do, do it all for the glory of God.' If we are to grow as Christians, we need to put our faith into practice.

The 'sleep' card reminds us that we mustn't get so busy that we stop having time with God. Psalm 46:10 says, 'Be still, and know that I am God', and Psalm 62:5 says, 'Yes, my soul, find rest in God; my hope comes from him.' If we are to grow in our healthy relationship with God, we need to spend time being quiet and enjoying being with him.

Just as we need certain things to maintain the healthy growth of our bodies, we need certain things to keep growing healthily as Christians.

Challenge

Explain that, at certain times in our lives, we make decisions about our physical health. We might feel a bit overweight, unfit or stressed and tired, so we decide to take actions such as eating more healthily, exercising more regularly or getting more relaxation.

Sometimes we need to do a spiritual health check, too. Ask the congregation to think about whether there are any areas where they might need to take action in their relationship with God. It may be reading their Bible or resting in God's presence, but, whatever it is, they will feel better when they begin to take action. Challenge them to take some action this week.

Week 18

USE YOUR TALENTS

Aim

Using the parable of the talents in Matthew 25, to encourage people to give their talents to God and allow him to use them

Bible links

- Matthew 25:14–30 (Parable of the talents)

You will need

- A very large cardboard box (for example, for a freezer or cooker)
- Small and large versions of a number of light objects (for example, a small and a large ball; a small sock and a huge Christmas stocking; a small and a large hat)
- A person to sit in the box
- A 10p, 50p or £1 coin
- Volunteers from the congregation who can demonstrate a special talent (such as hula hooping, juggling or playing a musical instrument) (optional).

NB: The parable of the talents is best told rather than read, as it can be quite a confusing passage.

Before the service, set the box up at the front of church. Arrange for your volunteer to sit in the box secretly, before the talk begins. If the box is large enough, the person may be able to sit on a chair without being seen. Also before the service, place the larger of each of the items into the box and make the volunteer aware of the order in which you are going to present the items. During the talk, you will be throwing the smaller item in and expecting the volunteer to throw the larger one straight back out.

Talk outline

If you have arranged for some people to show their talents, invite them to the front one at a time to perform. Ask the children to tell you about talents they have—things they are good at. Try to get a variety of answers, not just sport-related ones.

Explain that in the New Testament a 'talent' was a gold or silver disc. Show the 10p, 50p or £1 coin. The Greeks and Romans used silver coins called denarii as part of their monetary system. In Matthew 20:2 we read that one denarius was the wage for one day's work. One talent was worth about 6000 denarii.

Retell the parable of the talents from Matthew 25:14–30. (You may like to have this as the Bible reading before the all-age talk.) Make it clear that the first servant in the story received five talents, the next two talents and the last servant just one talent. They were all given different amounts of talents. Then, on his return, the master said exactly the same to the servant who had gained five more and two more talents: 'Well done, good and faithful servant! You have been faithful with a few things; I will put you in charge of many things. Come and share your master's happiness!' He was equally happy with both of them.

The master was angry with the third servant because he hadn't bothered to do anything with his talent; he had simply hidden it away. Explain that the parable talks about money but we can also use it to illustrate what happens with the talents and abilities we all have.

Show the congregation the small ball. Tell them to watch carefully as you throw the ball into the box. Timing here is quite important: when you throw the small ball in, the person inside the box needs to be ready to throw the large one out. (You may add sound effects.) Ask the children what happened. Repeat with another object. You could also ask volunteers to throw the objects into the box.

Explain that the box is an illustration of how God wants us to use all the gifts and talents he has given us. As we use them, they will increase and God will be able to use them more and more. Sometimes it can seem as if we only have one or two talents and other people have lots. In the parable, though, it made no difference to the master if a servant had five talents or two or even one. He was interested in what they did with the talents they had. In the same way, it doesn't matter to God whether we have one or 100 talents. What matters is how we use those talents.

Challenge

Ask the congregation to close their eyes for a few moments while they think of a talent that God has given them. It may be talking to people; it may be a sport; it may be baking; it may be DIY; it may be encouraging people. Challenge everyone to make a special effort to use their talent at least once during the coming week.

Week 19

STILL BELIEVING

Aim
To illustrate that faith, however small, is important to God, and to use the ascension to consider the disciples' faith once Jesus had returned to heaven

Bible links

- Acts 1:1–11; Luke 24:50–53; Mark 16:9–20 (Ascension)
- Acts 1:15; 2:1 (Followers meet together)
- Acts 2:2–13 (Coming of the Holy Spirit)
- Hebrews 11:1 (What is faith?)

You will need

- A glass and a jug of water
- A cardboard circle cut slightly wider than the circumference of the glass
- A towel
- A helium balloon on a long thread (ideally, a red heart shape, to allow the idea of God's love to be brought into the talk)

In advance of the talk, practise this water trick. Pour water into the glass until it is almost full. Place the cardboard circle over the glass and press lightly on it, ensuring that no air can get under the circle. Holding the circle firmly in place, tip the glass upside down and then slowly withdraw the hand that is holding the circle. The circle should remain in place with the water inside.

Talk outline

Ask the children if they can remember how long ago we celebrated Easter. Explain that after Jesus had been raised from the dead, he spent time with his friends and family before being taken up to heaven. Explain that we call this the 'ascension' of Jesus, and we celebrate it 40 days after Easter Day.

Read or retell Acts 1:7–9, emphasising verse 9: 'He was taken up before their very eyes, and a cloud hid him from their sight.'

Ask the children to come to the front and ask one of them to let go of the helium balloon. Watch as it floats up towards the ceiling. Just as the children watched the balloon until it hit the ceiling, so the disciples watched until Jesus was hidden by a cloud.

Ask the children how they think the disciples must have felt when Jesus left them. Remind them that Jesus had recently been killed and that many of the authorities wanted to get rid of Jesus' followers. No doubt the disciples were frightened. No doubt they were wondering what they should do next.

Ask for a volunteer and show them the glass. Explain that you are going to fill it with water and you want them to stand there while you hold it above their head and turn it upside down. Ask how they feel about that and whether they would rather not volunteer, after all. Ask them if they feel slightly worried.

Explain that you want to show the congregation something amazing. Pour water into the glass until it is almost full, place the card circle over the glass, slowly turn it upside down and remove your hand from the card. (You may want to keep your volunteer at the front as you do this but it is recommended that you check the trick is working before you place the glass over a volunteer's head.) Point out that everyone has now seen this amazing trick and therefore they know that it works. Ask if anyone wants to walk under the glass if you raise it higher in the air. Some of the children or young people will volunteer, so allow them to walk under the glass. Build up tension by saying, 'Carefully, carefully', 'Walk very, very slowly' and so on.

Say that although everyone saw the trick and even knew the person who was carrying it out, not everyone wanted to walk under the glass. Some people had the faith to walk under and others were not sure about it.

The Bible says a lot about 'faith'. Hebrews 11:1 says, 'Now faith is being sure of what we hope for and certain of what we do not see' (NIV 1984). Those people who walked under the glass hoped that the water wouldn't all pour on to their heads. They were also pretty sure that although they didn't really understand what they were seeing, they could trust the person who was doing the trick.

When Jesus was on earth, his disciples travelled with him and constantly saw miracles and listened to his teaching. It was easy for them to trust him when he was there. When Jesus went back to heaven, the disciples were suddenly left on their own. They could no longer see Jesus and they had to have faith that he was still with them and would still protect them. Throughout the years since Jesus went back to heaven, Christians have had to have faith that Jesus is alive and real, and that he is in heaven. We can't see him.

Read or retell Acts 1:10–11. The men in white clothing told the disciples that Jesus would one day come back to earth. It takes faith to believe this. It has been more than 2000 years since this promise was made, but Christians believe that one day it will happen. In the meantime, God has sent the Holy Spirit to live in the followers of Jesus (Acts 2:1–13). The Holy Spirit gives us faith to believe all that Jesus said.

Sometimes we might feel that our faith in God is very small. However, Jesus knew that we would often feel like that, so he used a very special illustration. In Matthew 17:20, he says, 'If you have faith as small as a mustard seed, you can say to this mountain, "Move from here to there" and it will move. Nothing will be impossible for you.'

Challenge

Challenge the congregation to spend a few minutes in the coming week remembering that Jesus is now in heaven. He is not dead but he is alive. Read Jesus' final words to the disciples recorded in Matthew's Gospel (28:18–20). Emphasise that he is with us always, to the very end of the age. Challenge the congregation to think about how the presence of Jesus with us should have an impact on our lives.

Week 20

USE YOUR TIME

Aim

To demonstrate that time is precious and we need to make the most of opportunities in our lives

Bible links

- Ecclesiastes 3:1–8 (A time for everything)
- Ecclesiastes 12:1 (Remember God while you are young)

You will need

- A variety of instruments for telling the time (wall clock, watch, stopclock, alarm clock, egg timer, mobile phone, sundial and so on)
- Prearranged reader for Ecclesiastes 3:1–8

Talk outline

Show the children each clock in turn and ask where they might see it and what it would be specifically used for. (For example, a wall clock would be in a house, workplace, school or church; a stopwatch is used for recording times in sport; an egg timer is used when boiling eggs, and so on.) Ask why we need to be able to tell the time, and why we need clocks at all.

Tell the congregation that you have some interesting facts about time that they might find quite shocking.

- The average person spends one-third of their lives asleep. This means that a nine-year-old will have slept for three years; a 32-year-old will have slept for approximately ten years, a 60-year-old for 20 years, and so on.

- The average adult will have spent approximately one-twelfth of their lives eating. This means that a 32-year-old will have spent about three years eating, a 48-year-old about four years and a 72-year-old about six years.

- The average adult will have spent approximately one-eighth of their lives watching television. So a 32-year-old will have spent about four years, a 40-year-old about five years and an 80-year-old about ten years.

- The average adult will have spent approximately one-sixteenth of their lives waiting in a queue, including waiting at traffic lights. A 32-year-old will have spent two years of their life in a queue, and a 64-year-old four years.

If we think about a 32-year-old, this all means that they will have spent almost 19 years of their life sleeping, eating, watching TV and waiting in a queue. Point out that sleeping and eating are essential, most of us would not wait in queues if we could help it, and there is nothing wrong with watching TV—it is important to relax. The figures do, however, make us think about how we use our time.

Ask the children to calculate how much time the 32-year-old would have had left for other activities (32 − 19 = 13 years). Ask them what they like to do best in their spare time. Explain that the Bible speaks about time.

Ask the volunteer to read Ecclesiastes 3:1–8: 'There is a time for everything, and a season for every activity under the heavens: a time to be born and a time to die…'

Show the children where the book of Ecclesiastes is found in the Bible, and show them where the words that have just been read are placed. Explain that, a few chapters further on, the writer talks about time again.

Read Ecclesiastes 12:1: 'Remember your Creator in the days of your youth…' (You may wish to read further.)

Ask the children and young people why they think the writer would tell them to remember God while they are still young. Isn't it more important for old people to remember God? Explain that if we begin to follow God with our lives now, we are more likely to continue to follow God later. By following God now, we can save ourselves from a lot of trouble, because the best way through life is to stay close to God and live in his way.

Ask the children and young people what they could do to help themselves remember God each day. Maybe they could get some Bible reading notes and read the Bible every day; maybe they could take time each evening before they climb into bed to pray and remember what God has done for them; maybe they could write out the words of Ecclesiastes 12:1 and stick them on the wall by their bed to remind them to remember God always.

Ask the rest of the congregation what they can do to help themselves remember God in every situation. Although the Bible encourages the young to remember God, it also encourages older people to do the same.

Read Hebrews 12:1–3 as a special message to the adults. We need to keep our eyes fixed on Jesus, throwing off whatever hinders us as we keep remembering God throughout our lives.

Challenge

Challenge the children and young people to think of something that will help them remember God every day. Challenge the older members of the congregation never to give up, but to keep their eyes on Jesus.

Week 21

ALWAYS LOOKING

Aim
To aid the understanding of the story of the lost sheep

Bible link

- Luke 15:1–7 (The lost sheep)

This talk can also fit with any of the lost and found stories in Luke 15.

You will need

- Sheep cut out of white paper—a few for each child (simple cloud shapes about 5cm across are adequate)
- One identical 'lost' sheep
- A container
- Party blowers
- Music (optional)

Before the service begins, place the paper sheep all over the church. Don't make them too difficult to find. Put some under chairs so that you can encourage the adults to join in with finding them. Secretly give the 'lost' sheep to a particular person, with instructions not to reveal this sheep until the appropriate part of the service.

Talk outline

Pretend you are listening hard. Ask the congregation if they can hear anything. Invite a few children to the front and ask if they can hear anything unusual. Ask if they can hear any 'baa-ing'. Say that you had a lot of sheep with you when you arrived this morning but unfortunately they have got scattered all over the church. Ask the children if they would be willing to help you find them. Explain that they can only collect one sheep at a time and must come and place the sheep in a container at the front before going to look for another sheep.

When you are ready, count down from five and start the music (or have the hunt going on during a song). Encourage the adults to call out if they have a sheep under their chair, so that the children can collect them and place them in the bowl. When you feel that enough time has elapsed, stop the music and ask the children to sit down.

Begin to take out the sheep one by one (quite quickly if there are a lot of sheep). Once you have looked at all the sheep in the container, shake your head, mutter, 'Oh dear, oh dear', wipe a tear away and explain that you feel unhappy because you know that one of your sheep is missing. You can't find it in the container. Ask the children what they think you should do. Should you look for it or should you just forget it, as it doesn't really matter about one sheep when you have so many?

State that you already have all these sheep, so to some people it may not matter at all that one is missing. However, to you it matters a great deal. Announce that you are going to have a look for the lost sheep.

Search all over the church. You may like to call out, 'Here, sheepy, sheepy', or stop a few times and ask the children if they think you should give up. Eventually move to the person with whom you 'planted' the sheep earlier and act surprised as you 'find' it. Suddenly shout, 'It's here! I've found it!'

Pretend that you are very excited. You may want to get the children to join in cheering, or place the sheep on your shoulder and carry it to the front. Tell the children you are so thrilled that you want to hold a huge party to celebrate. You thought this sheep was lost for ever, but you've found it. Give each child a party blower so that they can join in with the celebration.

Calm things down and explain that, in the Bible, Jesus tells a story about a lost sheep. The shepherd looked everywhere for this sheep, even though he had 99 others safely locked away in a sheep pen. Eventually, when the shepherd found the sheep, he lifted it up, placed it on his shoulders and carried it back home.

Explain that God calls us his sheep and calls himself the shepherd. God loves it when we stay close to him, but sometimes we wander away and do things that make God (and ourselves) sad. However, no matter what we have done wrong, God wants us to be close to him, so he goes out to look for us and always longs to welcome us back to himself. Isn't it wonderful to know that God will never stop loving us and will never give up looking for us?

Challenge

Give each of the children a few sheep and challenge them to place them somewhere in their house to remind themselves of the story during the week. You could encourage the children to play the game at home with their parents or other children and then explain the story to them.

Week 22

THREE IN ONE

Aim

To aid the understanding of the Trinity—one God in three persons. This could be tied to the story of Pentecost

Bible links

- Matthew 28:19 (the great commission)
- 2 Corinthians 13:13 (the Grace)
- John 14:26 (the promise of the Holy Spirit)
- Matthew 3:16–17 (Jesus' baptism)

You will need

- A triangle (musical instrument or triangle shape), a tricycle, a clover and a tripod, covered or placed in a large bag
- Matthew 28:19 written in large letters

In advance, try to find an adult volunteer who is related to three other people present in the service—for example, a woman who is a mother, wife and daughter to people in the room, or a man who is brother, son and uncle to people in the room. If the three other people can't be present, you could use photographs of them or simply ask the volunteer to name them.

Talk outline

Start the talk by asking for another volunteer to pull an object from the bag and hold it up so that everyone can see it. Ask what the object is and then invite someone to describe it. Repeat this for each object in the bag.

Ask if anyone can spot the link between the objects. The answer is the number three: the triangle has three sides, the tricycle has three wheels, the clover has three leaves, and the tripod has three legs. Ask if any of the children can work out what 'tri' means. If they can't, you may like to give clues by pointing out the different aspects of the triangle, tricycle and tripod. The prefix 'tri' means 'three'. Ask if other members of the congregation can think of other words beginning with 'tri'. You may want to record them on paper or on screen. Examples could be triple, triplets, trigonometry, and so on.

Ask if anyone under the age of eleven knows what the Trinity is. If you don't get much response, open the question up to the rest of the congregation (be careful not to ask someone who will give a long-winded theological answer). Explain that Christians use the word 'Trinity' to describe God. Although Christians believe that there is only one God, they believe that this one God is made of three separate persons—God the Father, God the Son and God the Holy Spirit—the Trinity.

Lift each object in turn and point out that there are three sides but one triangle, three wheels but one bike, three leaves but one clover, and three legs but one tripod.

Ask your prearranged volunteer to come forward. Does anyone know someone in the room who might be related to this person? Invite the first relative to come and stand next to the person. Repeat until three relatives are standing at the front. Point out that the volunteer is a mother, wife and daughter [change as necessary] but there is only one volunteer.

Explain that, with the Trinity, there is one God but three parts. The person standing at the front doesn't have one part of her that is only a mother or only a daughter. The whole of this woman is a mother, the whole of her is a daughter and the whole of her is a wife [change as necessary]. Likewise with the Trinity: God the Father is fully God, Jesus is fully God and the Holy Spirit is fully God.

Read or retell the story of Jesus' baptism in Matthew 3:13–17. Place particular emphasis on the words in verses 16 and 17: 'At that moment heaven was opened, and he saw the Spirit of God descending like a dove and alighting on him. And a voice from heaven said "This is my Son, whom I love; with him I am well pleased."' In these verses we see the presence of God the Father, God the Son and God the Holy Spirit.

Ask someone to read Matthew 28:19 (written beforehand in large letters): 'Therefore go and make disciples of all nations, baptising them in the name of the Father, and of the Son and of the Holy Spirit.' Point out that the verse says 'name of' not 'names of'. There is one God but three persons.

Ask the children if they can manage to be in two places at once. For example, could they be here in church and at home at the same time? Could they be at the park and in the swimming pool at the same time? When Jesus was on earth, he could only be in one place at a time. When he went back to heaven, his friends the disciples were very sad and frightened, but then something amazing happened. The disciples were locked in an upstairs room when suddenly God sent the Holy Spirit (see Acts 2: tell the story in more detail if this talk is used at Pentecost).

The experience changed their lives for ever. Now the Holy Spirit lived in them and would be there for ever. Emphasise that we never need to feel as if we are totally on our own because, just as he did then, God the Father sends the Holy Spirit to live in Jesus' followers today.

Challenge

Challenge the congregation to thank God for being with them as they get out of bed on every morning of the coming week, and to ask God to help them to live in a way that shows other people that the Holy Spirit lives within us.

You may want to challenge the children to find as many words as they can with 'tri' in them and give you the list when they come to church next week.

Week 23

WHO AM I?

Aim
To illustrate that there were clues that led Peter to realise who Jesus was

Bible links

- Matthew 16:13–20; Mark 8:27–30; Luke 9:18–22 (Peter's declaration)
- 2 Kings 2:1–14 (Elijah goes to heaven)

You will need

- The names of three or four famous people (can be fictional characters) written on large pieces of paper
- Stickers showing the names of famous people (optional)

Talk outline

Ask the children to take a good look at you. You may want to invite them to the front to look more closely. Ask the question, 'Who do you think I am?' Some of them may say your name; some may say your job; others may identify you as somebody's relative.

Explain that you are going to play a guessing game. You are going to pretend to be a famous person and you want a volunteer to guess who you are. The volunteer can only ask questions that can be answered by saying 'yes' or 'no'.

Invite a volunteer forward (choose an adult for the first go). Ask the volunteer to turn away while you show the rest of the congregation the name of the famous person written on the paper (make sure no one says it out loud). Now ask the volunteer to begin to guess. For example:

- Are you a man? No
- Are you a woman? Yes
- Are you a pop star? No
- Are you a sports star? No
- Are you a TV personality? No
- Are you a member of the royal family? Yes
- Are you young? No
- Are you the Queen? Yes

Be prepared for it to take many more guesses than this. Once the volunteer has guessed correctly, ask further volunteers to come forward, to guess the other three famous people. You may want to make it a competition to see which of the four volunteers can guess correctly in the lowest number of turns.

(If the number of people present is small, this talk can work well if each person has a sticker on their back, with the name of a famous person written on it. They then move round, asking questions with 'yes/no' answers to different people in the congregation as they try to guess the name of the person on their own back. An alternative is to place stickers on the backs of a few people and ask them to walk round asking a variety of people 'yes/no' questions until they have guessed the correct answer.)

Explain that Jesus once asked exactly the same question as you've been asking today. Read Matthew 16:13–16 or retell the story. Jesus first asked the disciples, 'Who do people say I am?' At the time, it seems that people in the crowds were all busily discussing the miracles that Jesus was doing and the things he was teaching. As the people talked about him, they were trying to make up their minds who Jesus could possibly be. Some people said that he was John the Baptist. John had recently been killed and some people hoped he had come back to life again. Some people thought Jesus was the prophet Elijah. Elijah had been taken up to heaven without dying (see 2 Kings 2:1–14), and a prophecy in Malachi 4:5, at the end of our Old Testament, had stated that Elijah would return. Other people thought that Jesus was Jeremiah or one of the other prophets from long ago. The people were trying to fit together all the clues: he healed people, he was a great teacher, he talked about God in a way that amazed the people, and so on.

Once Jesus had listened to the disciples' answers to what people were saying about him, he then asked them the question, 'But what about you? Who do you say I am?' Peter immediately jumped in with an answer. He said, 'You are the Christ, the son of the living God!'

Explain that, at this point, Peter didn't understand everything about Jesus. There are many clear indications in the Bible, after this statement, that he didn't fully understand the whole story. At this moment, though, he has seen enough to know that there is only one true explanation for who Jesus is: he really is the promised Messiah. Jesus tells Peter that one day he will be the leader of the church and calls him the rock on which the church will be built.

Ask the congregation who they think Jesus is. Many people would say he is a good man, a good example, or even a man sent from God. However, here we see that Jesus is far more than any of these.

Challenge

Challenge the congregation to take time to think about their answer to this question during the week. Who is Jesus? If he is who Peter says he is—the Christ, the Son of the living God—then that should make a big difference to our lives.

Week 24

SIGNPOSTS

<table>
<tr><td align="center">**Aim**</td></tr>
<tr><td align="center">To use road signs to illustrate that the Bible is a signpost guiding us in our lives. This talk could tie in with a service on the ten commandments</td></tr>
</table>

Bible links

- Colossians 3:12–16 (How we should live)
- Exodus 20:1–21 (Ten commandments)
- Psalm 119:105 (God's word is a light)

You will need

- Four pieces of card bearing the instructions 'Please can you stand up', 'Sit down', 'Put both hands in the air', 'Shout "hello!"'
- Instruction manual for something that can be put together during the talk (or any manual)
- Recipe book
- Unusual mixture of ingredients in a bowl (optional)

- A variety of road signs printed, drawn or displayed on screen (for example, no entry, falling rocks, roadworks, one way)
- Psalm 119:105 written out large enough for everyone to see
- A volunteer to read Colossians 3:12–13

Talk outline

As you begin the talk, hold the 'Please can you stand up' card in the air and show it to the entire congregation. (You may want to prime some people before the service, so that they quickly follow your instructions.) Allow enough time for the majority of the congregation to stand and then show the 'Sit down' card. Repeat with the other two instruction cards.

Ask the children to explain why people just stood up, sat down, raised their hands or shouted 'hello'. Ask if they can think of instructions they receive every day. Examples could be 'get up', 'get dressed', 'hold my hand' (while crossing a road), 'brush your teeth', 'be quiet', and so on. Ask what would happen if we took no notice of the instructions we are given.

Explain that you are going to talk about some other instructions. Show the instruction manual and ask someone to come to the front to read what the instructions are for. If possible, ask a number of volunteers to follow the instructions in the manual, to put together the item while you continue to talk (it might be a very simple model plane or a fold-up box). If you are just showing the manual, ask what could happen if you didn't have any instructions. If possible, tell a funny story about putting together a flatpack kit.

Show the recipe book. Ask what would happen if people just put any ingredients together in a pan or bowl when they were cooking. (You may like to demonstrate by placing an unusual variety of ingredients into a bowl, such as marmite, flour, chillies and so on. Invite a child to stir the mixture and ask the congregation if they think they would like to eat it— but don't let them.) It is important to follow the instructions in recipes if we are to get good results when baking.

Say that you are now going to show some other instructions that we often see when we are outside. Show each road sign in turn and ask people what they mean. Ask the children why we need these road signs. Ask what would happen if we didn't take any notice of what they said.

Pick up the Bible and point out that it is full of God's special instructions for us. It is a special message from God that will help and guide us in every part of our lives.

Sometimes, in the Bible, God tells us *not to do* certain things. The Bible says 'don't steal', 'don't lie', and so on. This doesn't mean that God is a spoilsport; it shows that God wants our lives to be the best and most enjoyable possible. (If you are using the ten commandments as a base for this talk, include more detail about the commandments here.)

Sometimes the Bible tells us *to do* certain things. Ask someone to read Colossians 3:12–13. In this passage God gives us instructions for how he wants us to live our lives.

Hold up Psalm 119:105: 'Your word is a lamp for my feet, a light on my path.' Ask the congregation to read it with you.

Say that if we want God to guide us in our lives, we need to take the time to read his instruction book.

Challenge

Challenge the children to learn Psalm 119:105 and repeat it to you next week.

Challenge the entire congregation to read part of God's instruction book every day this week. You may like to suggest that the whole congregation reads the same passage each day (keep it short). You could have cards ready to give out, with the suggested passages written on them. Challenge families to read the passages together each day.

Week 25

HOW HARD IS YOUR HEART?

<table>
<tr><td>

Aim

To demonstrate that we need to have soft hearts that will listen to what God says and act upon it

</td></tr>
</table>

Bible links

- Mark 6:52; 8:17 (The disciples' hard hearts)
- Hebrews 3:7–8 (Don't harden your heart)
- Ezekiel 11:19; 36:26 (Heart of stone or a soft heart)

You will need

- A collection of hard and soft objects mixed together in a large bag (for example, sponge, towel, cotton wool, jumper, cushion and cuddly toy; rock, glass, metal spoon, piece of wood and plastic spatula)
- The words 'hard' and 'soft' written on large pieces of paper

Talk outline

Show the congregation the bag full of objects and ask for two volunteers to hold up the two cards with 'hard' and 'soft' written on them. Ask them to stand a few metres apart.

Explain that you need volunteers to come to the front to take one item out of the bag and decide whether it should be placed under the 'hard' or 'soft' banner. As each item is selected, ask a few questions such as, 'What is it? What would you use it for? Is it hard or soft?' Ask the volunteer to go and stand next to the correct description, holding the item so that the rest of the congregation can see it.

When all of the items have been placed under the correct banner, ask if anyone can describe any differences between the hard and soft items. Answers could include warm/cold, comfortable/uncomfortable, squidgy/firm, and so on.

Ask what would happen if you were to place any of the items in a bucket of water. Someone will answer that the water would run off the hard items but the soft ones would soak it up. Demonstrate this with a few items if possible.

Ask the volunteers to sit down while you tell a well-known story. If possible, allow the children to sit at the front and hold on to the hard/soft objects. Tell the story of the feeding of the 5000, as found in Mark 6:30–44. Ask people to imagine how they would have felt if they had just seen such an amazing miracle. Ask them what they would have thought about Jesus.

Although the disciples had been part of the amazing miracle, they didn't seem to understand or be able to take in what they had just seen. Straight after this miracle, Jesus put his disciples in a boat while he went off to pray. A few hours later, during a fierce storm, Jesus appeared to them walking on the water of the lake, and they were terrified. Mark 6:51–52 says that the disciples were amazed because they hadn't understood what had happened with the loaves and the fishes when 5000 people had been fed.

Ask someone to read out Mark 6:51–52: 'Then Jesus climbed into the boat with them, and the wind died down. They were completely amazed, for they had not understood about the loaves; their hearts were hardened.'

Explain that, after this event, the disciples saw Jesus healing many people. Some people even touched the edge of Jesus' cloak and were healed. The disciples saw deaf, blind, mute and paralysed people healed and even saw another miracle involving food, where 4000 people were fed from seven loaves. Even so, they struggled to believe. In Mark 8:17–18, Jesus asks, 'Do you still not see or understand? Are your hearts hardened? Do you have eyes but fail to see, and ears but fail to hear? And don't you remember?'

Explain that the Bible often talks about people having hard hearts. Just as water would roll off the pile of hard things, so some people hear about God and the words just 'roll off' them. You might describe it as 'going in one ear and out of the other'. They never really stop to think about what they have heard and they certainly don't allow it to enter their lives and change them. God wants us to have soft hearts that 'soak in' everything we hear about him. He wants us not only to take in what he says, but also to put it into action in our lives.

Sometimes, things can happen in our lives that make us unhappy or scared, and they can make us feel hardened towards God. We don't understand why things happen, so we stop listening to God. Perhaps we stop reading the Bible and stop coming to church. Sometimes we still do these things but we put up a barrier inside ourselves, so that nothing we hear really gets through to our hearts. The good news, though, is that God can change our hearts.

Read Ezekiel 11:19b and 36:26b. Explain that if we feel as if we are hard towards God and are not listening to him, we can ask God to soften our hearts and he promises that he will do so.

Challenge

Challenge the congregation to spend a moment every morning this week asking God to give them a soft heart during that day. As they ask God to soften their heart, they can look for ways in which it happens. It may be that they understand something new about God, or it may be that their feelings or attitudes to another person begin to change.

Week 26

ALWAYS AVAILABLE

Aim
To show that God is always there to listen to us at any time of the day or night

Bible links

- Psalm 121:3–4 (God does not sleep)
- Deuteronomy 31:6; Matthew 28:20 (God will never leave us)
- Psalm 145:18 (God is near when we call)

You will need

- A mobile phone
- A volunteer to knock on the door and ask if they can speak with you
- A volunteer dressed as a postman, with a parcel
- A volunteer to ring your phone at a prearranged moment in the service

For this talk to work well, it is essential that the timing is correct. The three volunteers involved need to be certain of when to carry out their parts.

Talk outline

If there is room, ask the children to come and sit at the front. This means that they will definitely hear your mobile phone, see your shocked face, and so on.

Begin to chat to the children about their week. After a moment, there should be a loud knocking on a door. As everyone turns round to see what is happening, the volunteer should walk towards you and begin to talk in a loud voice, saying something of very little importance—for example, 'Sorry to disturb you, but I could really do with having a chat about what you want to eat a week on Friday, when you come round for tea. I was thinking that maybe we could eat…' Respond by saying that you're very sorry but you are a bit busy and could he please talk to you another time? The volunteer looks disappointed and leaves the room.

As soon as he or she has left, the 'postman' should march to the front of church and ask you to sign for the parcel he is carrying. Tell him you would rather he didn't interrupt as you are in the middle of doing something and it is rude just to walk in on you. The postman should pull a face, moan a bit and eventually agree to come back later.

Begin to talk to the children again, apologising that you have been interrupted twice. Explain that it shouldn't happen again and you are very sorry. As soon as you've said this, your phone should ring. The person dialling the number needs to allow the phone to ring for long enough to cause a bit of a disturbance as you try to find it in your pocket. Eventually, pretend to answer it and roll your eyes as you say something like, 'No, thank you, I do not want double glazing, car insurance or a new boiler.' Put the phone back in your pocket, looking cross.

Apologise again to the congregation, explaining that usually you turn off your mobile before the service, it is very unusual for people to barge into church in such a rude manner, and you will try to make sure it doesn't happen again.

Ask the children if they have ever been cross when they've been interrupted. Maybe they were watching a favourite programme on television and they had to go out shopping. Maybe they were in the middle of a game when they had to stop for tea. All of us get cross when we are interrupted at an inappropriate moment or when we are in the middle of something we enjoy. Often, children interrupt things too. Perhaps a parent is making tea and a child keeps asking for things and is eventually told to go away. Perhaps a child won't go to sleep and keeps coming downstairs or into a parent's bedroom and is told to go back to bed. Perhaps adults are having a conversation and a child is told to go into the other room and stop interrupting.

However, with God it is different. God will never ever tell us to go away. It doesn't matter what time of the day or night it is. It doesn't matter if we've told him about our problem or asked him to help us a hundred times every day: he will still always be there to listen to us. In fact, he loves us to talk to him at any time, in any place.

Read Psalm 121:3–4: 'He who watches over you... will neither slumber nor sleep.' The Bible tells us that God never goes to sleep but watches over us every day and every night. He is always there for us to talk to at any time.

Read Psalm145:18: 'The Lord is near to all who call on him.' As soon as we call out to God (as soon as we pray), God is close to us.

Remind the congregation of how you felt when you were interrupted. You sent away the person who interrupted, the postman and the person on the phone because you didn't want to talk to them at that particular moment. Emphasise again that, with God, there is never a 'bad moment' to contact him. He will always be there to listen.

Challenge

Challenge the congregation to stop for a moment, the next time they feel cross because someone has interrupted them, and remember that God is never too busy for them. Challenge the children to thank God, each time they lie down to go to sleep, that he will be with them all through the night because he never needs to sleep.

Week 27

APPEARANCES CAN BE DECEPTIVE

Aim

To demonstrate that what people look like on the outside isn't always a good indication of what they are really like on the inside

Bible links

- 1 Samuel 16:1–13 (Samuel anoints David)
- John 7:24 (Stop judging by appearances)

You will need

- A blindfold
- Three packets of crisps with distinctive flavours (for example, salt and vinegar; barbecue; cheese and onion)

Before the service, open each packet carefully and swap the contents, so that each packet contains a different flavour from the one shown on the outside. The congregation must not be able to tell that the packets have been tampered with. (Opening at the back seam usually gives the best results.)

Talk outline

To start your talk, ask if any children have a favourite flavour of crisps. Ask them to name as many flavours as they can think of. Ask for a volunteer (adult or youth) who likes eating crisps, doesn't mind being blindfolded and is good at distinguishing between different flavours.

With your crisp packets still hidden, blindfold your volunteer. Explain to those watching that they must keep very quiet. They mustn't read the variety of crisp out loud and they mustn't say if the volunteer is right or wrong until the end of the testing.

Open the first crisp packet and show the congregation the flavour. Now ask the blindfolded volunteer to take a crisp (guide their hand into the packet if necessary), chew it carefully and name the flavour. Don't tell them whether they are right or wrong. You may like to ask someone to write down the answer given.

Repeat for each of the flavours, then remove the blindfold and show the volunteer the packets. The volunteer may seem very surprised that they got it wrong. Ask them why they think they got it wrong. Ask the congregation if anyone thinks they could have done better.

Point out that, actually, the volunteer has done much better than it appears. Explain that before the service began, you swapped all the contents of the packets round. The volunteer was correct each time and those watching were the ones who were wrong about the contents of each bag.

When the congregation saw the outside of the crisp packets, they thought they knew what flavour the crisps inside would be. In the same way, we often see what people look like on the outside and assume that we know what they are like on the inside. We may look at someone old and think they don't understand what it is like to be young; we may see someone who wears lovely clothes and assume that they are a good, kind person, or someone who looks different in some way and assume that they are unpleasant or bad.

In John 7:24, Jesus says, 'Stop judging by appearances.' His words are still very important for us today.

A story in the Bible (in 1 Samuel 16) tells us about a time when Samuel the prophet was told by God to go and choose the future king of Israel. Samuel went to the house of a man called Jesse, where he met each of seven brothers in turn. Each of them looked good. However, God had other plans. God spoke to Samuel and said, 'Don't look on the outward appearance, because man looks on the outside but God looks at the heart.' Instead, God chose the youngest boy, who, at the time, simply sat on the hillside watching his father's sheep. Samuel would not have thought of the boy David as the man whom God had chosen to be a great king. But God saw something different in David: he saw not what David was, but what David could become.

Ask everyone to look round at the people in church or, perhaps, to stand and say 'hello' to those close by. All of us are different. We have different coloured eyes and hair. Some of us are old and some of us young. Some of us like the way we look and some of us wish we looked different. When God looks at us, he sees what we are like on the inside. He sees if we love him and he sees how we care about other people. God knows that these things are far more important than our outward appearance.

Challenge

Ask the children and youth to think about someone at school that they find it hard to like. (Don't ask them to name the person.) Challenge them to try to look for something good in that person this week. You might even challenge them to mention the 'good thing' if other children are being nasty or talking unkindly about that particular person.

Challenge the wider congregation to do the same with someone that they find it difficult to like.

Week 28

BEING IMITATORS

Aim
To emphasise that we don't need to follow other people but, rather, should be imitators of God

Bible links

- Ephesians 5:1 (Imitate God)
- 1 Peter 1:14–16 (Be holy)
- Matthew 16:24 (Follow Jesus)
- 1 John 2:3–4 (Keep his commandments)
- 1 Peter 2:21 (Walk in Jesus' steps)
- Hebrews 13:7 (Copy your leaders)

You will need

- Three small cards with different animal names on them (for example, monkey, snake, giraffe)
- Three small cards with different occupations on them (for example, dentist, hairdresser, fire-fighter)

- Three small cards with different actions on them (for example, making a bed, vacuuming the carpet, changing the wheel on a car)
- A prearranged volunteer

You can include any animal, job or action that is easy to act out. Use more cards if you wish.

Your volunteer should be prepared to be interviewed about his or her life, work or hobby while copying all your actions. To work best, these actions need to be made obvious and should include a comedy element.

Talk outline

Explain that you have some cards in your hand, with the names of different animals written on them. Ask for some volunteers to come to the front and do impressions of the animals. As each impression is carried out, allow the congregation to guess the name of the animal. Ask the volunteers to remain at the front while the other animal impressions are completed. Once all the animals have been correctly identified, ask the volunteers how they knew what to do. (You are expecting them to say that they have seen the animal in a zoo or book, or on television, and are imitating the actions they've seen.)

Explain that the next cards show different occupations. Invite volunteers to carry out the actions for the congregation to guess. As before, ask the volunteers to stay at the front until each occupation has been guessed correctly and then ask how they knew what actions to make. (You are expecting them to say that they have been to the dentist or hairdresser and can therefore copy their actions.)

Repeat with the everyday actions, again asking the volunteers how they knew what actions to do. You may like to discuss who they have seen making a bed/vacuuming/changing a wheel.

Say that you have arranged for someone in the congregation to tell everybody a bit about their life, job or hobby. Invite your volunteer to the front and ask their name. At the same time, make some sort of subtle action, such as scratching your head. The volunteer should immediately copy your action as they answer the question. Continue with your questions, making your actions less and less subtle so that it becomes obvious that the interviewee is copying everything you do. After a while, you may want to take it further and have the interviewee repeating everything you say. Try to make it as comical as possible, eventually doing or saying things so quickly that the volunteer has difficulty keeping up.

After a suitable length of time, send the volunteer back to their seat and ask the children what just happened. As they explain that the volunteer was copying everything you did and everything you said, point out that although it was funny when the volunteer copied you, there is a serious side to copying or imitating someone. Ask the children if they can think of times when copying someone else could be serious. Discuss times when it is wrong to copy—when people are doing something wrong or being unkind or rude. Discuss times when it could be good to copy—when people are doing the right things or being kind or sharing.

The Bible speaks about copying or imitating people. Say that you are going to read a few verses from the Bible and you want people to spot who we are told to copy in each verse.

Read Ephesians 5:1: 'Be imitators of God, therefore, as dearly loved children, and live a life of love, just as Christ loved us and gave himself up for us.' We need to follow Christ's example of love.

Read 1 Peter 2:21: 'To this you were called, because Christ suffered for you, leaving you an example, that you should follow in his steps.' We need to follow Jesus, even if it is hard and we 'suffer' for following him.

Explain that Paul was the writer of the letter to the Corinthians. Then read 1 Corinthians 11:1: 'Follow my example, as I follow the example of Christ.' Although we are ultimately to follow God, there are also people who set good examples that we can imitate. Paul lived a life that showed Jesus to the rest of the world.

Read Hebrews 13:7: 'Remember your leaders, who spoke the word of God to you. Consider the outcome of their way of life and imitate their faith.' Challenge the leaders in the congregation to consider whether they are living in a way that everyone should follow. Point out that we can all be leaders in this way—being good examples for others to copy.

Today, peer pressure has a massive impact on our lives. Whether we are children or adults, there is always pressure to join in with inappropriate things. As we get older, the pressure to strive for bigger and better possessions, to be more attractive, to be rich and famous, or to copy someone else's lifestyle and values, can often increase. The Bible asks us not to copy other people but to imitate Jesus.

Challenge

Challenge the congregation to spend time this week reading Philippians 2:1–16. Suggest that they read it every morning. (You may want to have the verses printed out on a bookmark for each person to keep.) This passage speaks about the attitude of Jesus. Challenge the congregation to put into practice (copy or imitate) what we read about Jesus in it.

Week 29

ALWAYS THE SAME

Aim
To illustrate that, while everything else in the world changes, God never changes

Bible links

- Hebrews 13:8 (Jesus remains the same)
- Malachi 3:6 (God does not change)
- Isaiah 40:8 (God's word lasts for ever)

You will need

- Pictures showing winter and summer (or all four seasons)
- The words of Malachi 3:6 and Hebrews 13:8 displayed on a screen or written out large enough to read
- A selection of the following:
  - ❖ A photograph of yourself (or another adult member of the congregation) as a baby and a recent photograph
  - ❖ A bunch of fresh flowers and a bunch of dead flowers

- ❖ An 'old fashioned' toy and a new toy
- ❖ A seed and a plant
- ❖ A Mars bar showing the price in the 1980s (16p in 1982) and one showing the current price
- ❖ Any other items that show change over time

Talk outline

Show the congregation the baby photograph and ask them to guess who it is. If it is of a member of the congregation, you may want to ask five people to stand up or come to the front and allow others to guess which of them the photograph shows. Then show an up-to-date photograph of the person. If possible, display the photos on a screen next to each other so that they can be clearly seen. Ask the children what the differences are between the two.

Show the congregation the two bunches of flowers and ask the children to spot the differences.

Show the old-fashioned and new toys and ask the children what the differences are. Continue with each of the items available.

Point out that all of these things have changed in some way over a period of time. The person has changed from a baby to an adult: they have grown older. The flowers that were once beautiful have now withered and died. The tiny seed has grown into a plant; the cost of food has gone up and up, and so on.

Show the children the pictures of the seasons. Ask them to describe the changes that take place every year. Explain that everything in our lives and everything in the world changes.

Sometimes change is good: none of us would want to stay as a baby for 70 years. Sometimes change is bad: food goes off and flowers die. Sometimes change can make us feel unsettled: we start school, we move house or we get married. Sometimes change can be stopped (we could decide not to move house) but often changes can't be prevented. We could care for the flowers, giving them fresh water and plant food, but ultimately they will still die.

The Bible teaches something about change. In the last book of the Old Testament we read something wonderful.

Ask someone to read Malachi 3:6: 'I the Lord do not change.' Ask the children and then the congregation to read it together.

Ask someone to read Hebrews 13:8: 'Jesus Christ is the same yesterday and today and for ever.' Ask the children and then the congregation to read it together.

In a world that is always changing, it is wonderful to know that one thing remains the same. This means that everything we learn about God or Jesus in the Bible is as true today as it always has been. God is the creator; he is all-powerful, he can do anything. He can heal, he can forgive, he is always there, he always listens, he always loves us and he always cares for us. This would be wonderful if it was only for today—but it is true for ever.

Challenge

Challenge the congregation to learn the words of Hebrews 13:8: 'Jesus Christ is the same yesterday and today and for ever.' You may want to provide some small prizes for the children who can repeat it to you next week.

Challenge the congregation to remember this when things go wrong during the coming week. Even if everything else changes and things fall apart, God will never change and will always be there.

Week 30

WATCH YOUR TONGUE

Aim
To show that once words have been spoken, they can never be taken back again

Bible links

- James 3:1–12; Ephesians 4:29 (Controlling the tongue)

You will need

- A banana and a bowl
- A tube of toothpaste
- A large piece of paper on a board, tilted so that the congregation can see what is being drawn
- Floor covering
- The words of Ephesians 4:29 printed on paper

Before the service, give the printed words of Ephesians 4:29 to a child, to be read out later.

Talk outline

If many children are present, you may like to ask them to move to the front for this talk.

Ask for two volunteers. This activity often causes the congregation to laugh, so make sure you choose volunteers who will be comfortable with that. If necessary, use adults.

Say that you are hungry and you would like to eat some banana and ice cream. Explain that you want one of the volunteers to break the banana up and put it in the bowl, ready for you to eat.

While the first volunteer is breaking up the banana, give the second volunteer the toothpaste. Explain that you want them to draw a picture on the large piece of paper, using the toothpaste. Ask the rest of the congregation to try to guess what the picture is meant to be as the volunteer draws it. (If a child is drawing the picture and is unsure what to draw, whisper simple suggestions, such as a house, flower or car.)

While the picture is being drawn, turn your attention back to the volunteer with the banana. Pretend that you are no longer hungry and you have decided that it would be rude to eat in front of everybody. Casually ask the volunteer to put the banana back inside its skin so that you can eat it later. Then turn your attention back to the person drawing, but be aware that the volunteer with the banana will now be slightly confused, as they will realise they cannot do what you have asked them to do.

The first volunteer might try to piece the banana back together and cram it into its skin. If they don't immediately do this, encourage them by saying, 'You're going to have to piece all that back together. Can you fit it back in the skin? Would someone like to come to help?' and so on.

Wait until the second volunteer has completed the drawing and people have guessed what it is. Now casually ask the volunteer to put the toothpaste back into its tube, ready for you to use tonight when you brush your teeth. When the volunteer says that they can't do this, ask them to have a go or suggest that someone else comes to help them. Pretend that you are slightly worried, by asking questions like, 'How am I going to clean my teeth tonight?' or 'What if I get smelly breath?'

When you feel the time is right, admit that it is impossible to fit the banana back in its skin or the toothpaste back in its tube. Explain that, in the same way, when we say something and the words come out of our mouth, it is impossible to put them back in again. If we say something unkind to someone, they will remember it. We can say sorry and they may forgive us, but they will always know what we said and sometimes those words can stay with a person for the whole of their lives.

The Bible describes the tongue as a fire that can cause lots of damage. James 3:5–6 says, 'Consider what a great forest is set on fire by a small spark. The tongue also is a fire.' Ask the children what they think this means. Explain that even a tiny spark can set off a huge fire. (There may be recent news articles or pictures you could display on screen.) In the same way, something small that we say can cause a lot of damage.

Another verse in the Bible tells us that we shouldn't let bad talk come out of our mouths, but should only say things that will help other people. Ask your prearranged child volunteer to read Ephesians 4:29: 'Do not let any unwholesome talk come out of your mouths, but only what is helpful for building others up.' Ask them what they think the verse means. Explain that God wants us to make an effort to use our mouths to help other people. Ask the children if they remember anything that has been said to them that made them feel good. We can all say things that make people feel good inside.

Challenge

Challenge the whole congregation to make an effort this week to say three things to different people that will make those people feel good. It may be as simple as saying thank you for a lovely meal.

Week 31

RUNNING THE RACE

Aim
To illustrate that sometimes the Christian life can be hard work and we need to persevere rather than give up

Bible links

- Philippians 3:14; Galatians 6:9 (Press on towards the goal)
- Romans 5:3 (Suffering produces perseverance)

You will need

- Volunteers to act out the parts of an athlete (needs to be reasonably fit), a knitting champion (needn't be able to knit) and a Rubik cube expert (if possible, someone who can complete a Rubik cube quickly, but this is not essential)
- An unwanted jumper attached to two knitting needles (the jumper must have a huge hole in it)
- A Rubik cube

Talk outline

Announce that today you are privileged to have a very special athlete visiting. The athlete has been working extremely hard to improve their fitness and is going to show us what has been achieved. Ask everyone to give a big cheer and a round of applause. The athlete should jog to the front and begin to warm up (press-ups, star jumps, and so on). After one or two exercises, the athlete should stop and apologise, pointing out that they are not actually a famous athlete yet, but hope to be one in the future.

While the athlete continues to exercise, announce that you are also very privileged today to have the national knitting champion with you. Ask everyone to clap as the knitting champion comes forward. When they arrive at the front, they should apologise: they are not actually the champion yet, but hope to be so one day. They should hold up the jumper with the huge hole in it and explain that they still have a long way to go before they become a champion knitter, but they are trying hard.

As the knitter sits at the front and pretends to knit, the athlete could begin to jog round the church. At intervals the athlete should stop, wipe their brow and comment on what hard work it is. At intervals the knitter should make loud comments like, 'Oh no, I've dropped another stitch,' or 'Oh no, I've dropped all the stitches' as the jumper falls on the floor.

Announce that you want to introduce another champion. This time it is the Rubik cube champion, who should come to the front looking puzzled, holding a muddled cube. They should apologise and explain that they are not actually a Rubik cube champion, but would like to become one in the future. Their aim is to beat the world record of completing the cube in 5.5 seconds. (Even if this person can complete the cube, they should not do so at this point.)

While the athlete, knitter and Rubik cube solver continue to practise, ask the congregation if they think any of the 'champions' will ever achieve their goal. Ask why they think it is not really possible. Point out that, in life, it is good to have a goal. It's good to want to achieve something that is hard work and needs time, effort and patience.

The Bible speaks about having a goal. In Paul's letter to the Philippians, he says that he is pressing on towards a goal. He says, 'I press on towards the goal to win the prize for which God has called me heavenwards in Christ Jesus.' Paul doesn't mean a goal like a football goal; he is talking about pressing on through his life as he lives for God. There may be many struggles on the way; it won't always be easy, but Paul is going to press on until he arrives in heaven. In heaven he will receive the wonderful prize of being with God for ever.

Ask the athlete to stand next to you and point out how tired and sweaty the athlete looks. Training is not easy. It is very easy to give up, to eat too much and to have lots of days off. However, if someone is determined to be a top athlete, they will persevere and continue, despite the fact that they often feel like giving up.

Ask the knitter to stand by you. Point out that they have a lot of work to do if they are going to become a champion. Things will go wrong: they will drop stitches and may need to start all over again many times. However, if they are deter-mined, they will keep on persevering.

Ask the Rubik cube solver to stand by you. Say that sometimes, as they try to sort the cube out, it just seems to become a bigger mess. However, a determined person will keep on persevering and will eventually get there. At this point, the talk works best if the solver can spring into action and complete the cube so that everyone can see, but this is not essential.

Explain that living as a Christian can sometimes seem like hard work. Sometimes things go wrong. Often we can feel like giving up, and sometimes the more we try to sort things out, the more confused they become. However, the Bible encourages us to keep going, to persevere even when things get tough. Galatians 6:9 says, 'Let us not become weary in doing good, for at the proper time we will reap a harvest if we do not give up.'

Encourage the congregation to persevere in their Chris-tian life. Encourage them to keep trying, no matter what they are going through, knowing that God is faithful and is with them every step of the way.

Challenge

Ask the congregation to close their eyes and think of an area of their life that seems hard at the moment. Encourage them in the silence to ask God for the strength to carry on following him in this situation. Suggest that everyone prays that same prayer each morning this week.

Week 32

TEAMWORK

Aim

To show the importance of working together
as a team within the church

Bible links

- Philippians 2:1–5 (Looking to each other's interests)
- 1 Corinthians 1:10; 12:20–25; Acts 2:42–47 (Being united)

You will need

- Objects that represent teams (football shirt, netball bib, cricket bat and hockey stick) placed in a large bag
- Someone to read from the Bible
- A congregation member who takes part in a team sport and is happy to be interviewed (optional)

Talk outline

Ask for volunteers to come forward one at a time to select an object from the bag. As the object is selected, ask them to hold it in the air and ask people in the congregation to name the object and explain what it is used for. Once all the equipment has been identified, ask if anyone can explain what all the objects have in common. Someone will say that they are all pieces of sports equipment. Agree that this is true, but point out that there isn't a running machine or a cross-trainer or a trampoline, so what is it about sport that specifically ties these objects together? If necessary, give clues such as, 'Would I wear this netball bib on my own? Would I have a good game of cricket if all I had was a bat?' Continue until someone answers that all the objects are used for team sports.

Ask the object holders to return to their seats and ask for eight different volunteers: these people need to be sensible, willing to join in and also physically fit. Ask them to stand in a circle facing each other and then put one hand into the middle and hold hands with the person opposite. Now ask them to put their other hand into the middle and take hold of a different person's hand. Challenge them to untangle themselves without letting go of each other's hands until they are all standing in a complete circle. They can loosen their grip so that no one gets hurt but their hands must stay in contact the whole time. When they are unravelled, it is OK if some people are facing out of the circle.

As the volunteers untwist, give a running commentary to the congregation, pointing out who is suggesting what solution, who is stepping over whom, which person is the most tangled, and so on.

You could arrange for two teams to carry out the same activity at once, in competition—although care must be taken that people don't get carried away and hurt each other. If two teams are used, keep moving from team to team as you commentate.

Once the teams are untangled, ask the congregation for comments on how they performed. Did they work together well? Did someone take charge? If two teams took part, ask why one team won and not the other. Remember that you are looking for answers about teamwork and cooperation between people.

If you have arranged for a team player to be interviewed, ask them to come forward. This works well if the player can run forward in their team kit, possibly dribbling a ball or carrying a bat. Ask questions such as 'What sport do you play? How long have you done this for? Why do you play a team sport and not just go jogging? What is the most important thing about being in a team?'

The Bible has a lot to say about Christians working together as a team. There are many passages that could be used as examples of this. Ask the congregation to listen as someone reads out your chosen Bible passage. Ask them to listen specifically for how people are working as a team in the passage. For example, in Philippians 2:1–5 Paul encourages the Philippians to be like-minded, to have the same purpose, to be unselfish, to consider others, and so on.

Mention a few of the ways in which your own church demonstrates teamwork. Examples could include a recent project with many people involved, the number of people involved in the Sunday service, the team that keeps the church garden neat, the people on the coffee rota, and so on. Many people are needed to make the church run well. Point out how bad it would be if everyone simply thought about themselves and didn't consider others.

Ask if anyone has a favourite football team. The answers are almost guaranteed to include some with the word 'United' in them. (If not, then ask the congregation to name some famous football teams.) Ask why a football team would have the word 'united' in its name. Someone should answer that a team needs to be working together as one. Read the Oxford Dictionary definition of the word 'united': 'joined together for a common purpose, or by common feelings'.

Read out what Paul says in 1 Corinthians 1:10: 'I appeal to you, brothers and sisters, in the name of our Lord Jesus Christ, that all of you agree with one another in what you say and that there be no divisions among you, but that you be perfectly united in mind and thought.'

Challenge

There are many people involved in the church who aren't seen at the front but carry out important roles behind the scenes. Ask the congregation to think of a particular job, such as cleaning, making the coffee, tidying the garden or visiting people who are ill. Challenge them to find out who does one of these jobs and to make a special effort this week to thank them for what they do. By doing this you will encourage them as they carry out their teamwork.

Week 33

MEMORIES

Aim

To illustrate the meaning of the Communion service by considering the importance of memories

---

Bible links

- Matthew 26:17–30; Mark 14:12–26; Luke 22:7–23; John 13:1–17; 1 Corinthians 11:23–26 (Last Supper)

You will need

- Items that remind you (or other volunteers) of specific events (for example, a souvenir from a holiday; old school tie; wedding dress; war medals; a baby's first shoe)
- Bread and wine, as appropriate for the church's Communion tradition
- Onscreen pictures that will evoke memories in the older members of the congregation—for example, pictures of World War II, bygone actors or old advertisements

Talk outline

Show the congregation one item of your memorabilia and ask the children why they think it might be important enough for you to keep it. Repeat with your other items, each time explaining why you didn't want to throw the item away.

Alternatively, invite prearranged volunteers to come forward to share their memorabilia. Make sure their contributions are kept short: two or three sentences will be plenty.

Point out that each item holds special memories for the person who has shown it. When they look at the item it reminds them of a special occasion or a special person. Ask the children if they have anything precious that reminds them of something or someone special. (Remember to be sensitive: children could recently have lost a relative or pet.)

Ask for a volunteer who will respond appropriately to the following joke. You may want to arrange this with an adult in the congregation, or ask two young people or adults to tell the joke between them.

You: Will you remember me in five minutes?

Volunteer: Of course I will.

You: Will you remember me in an hour?

Volunteer: Yes.

You: Will you remember me in a day?

Volunteer: Yes, of course I will.

You: Will you remember me in a week?

Volunteer: Of course I will. You're pretty hard to forget.

You: Will you remember me in a year?

Volunteer: This is getting silly! Of course, I'll remember you
            for ever!

You: Knock, knock.

Volunteer: Who's there?

You: There you are, you've forgotten me already.

Point out that, although this is only a joke, in reality we do
often forget things. Ask if anyone in the congregation has
a special way of remembering things that are important.
Answers may include writing things on calendars, making
a list, tying a knot in a hanky (in years gone by), writing on
your hand, using sticky notes, and so on.

Jesus knew that we find it easy to forget, so he wanted
to do something to remind us of the most important event in
the world.

Tell the story of the Last Supper, reminding the children
that Jesus went to Jerusalem to celebrate the Passover with
his disciples. They went to an upstairs room and, while
everyone was reclining around the table, Jesus took the
bread, broke it and handed it round, saying, 'This is my
body given for you.' After this, Jesus handed round the
wine, saying, 'This is my blood, poured out for many for the
forgiveness of sins.'

Jesus used the bread and the wine that had been made
ready for the Passover celebration, but he suggested that it
symbolised something different. It represented the fact that
Jesus would die: his body would be broken and his blood
would be shed when he died on the cross. That may seem

like a sad thing to think about, but actually it is a wonderful thing. As Jesus said, his death brought forgiveness to people. Remind the children that Jesus is no longer dead but is alive again for ever.

Jesus wanted his disciples in biblical times and all his followers in the future to remember the most important thing about his life on earth—the fact that he died so they could be forgiven. Because of this, he told his disciples to continue to break the bread and drink the wine until he comes back again. Now Christians all over the world do this regularly to make sure they always remember what Jesus did for them.

The apostle Paul wrote about the importance of breaking bread, in 1 Corinthians 11:23–26. You may want to read these words, particularly if this talk is part of the Communion service.

Challenge

Challenge the congregation to find one piece of memorabilia this week and to spend a few minutes thanking God for the joy of the memories that it brings. Challenge them also to create good memories for the people they know.

Week 34

CREATION'S VARIETY

Aim

To show that God made a beautiful creation. We are all different and this is something wonderful to celebrate. This could be tied into the creation story or a 'Celebrating differences' service

---

Bible links

- Genesis 1—2 (Creation)
- Ephesians 2:10 (God's workmanship)

You will need

- A flipchart or clipboard for recording answers and someone to do the recording
- A selection of flowers
- Five cards with the name or picture of a different animal on each card
- A selection of toy animals or pictures of animals displayed on a screen

Talk outline

Show the congregation a flower that is easily identifiable and ask them its name. Ask one of the children to come out to the front to hold the flower. Explain that you want to make a list of as many different flowers as possible and you need two volunteers who think they may be good at naming flowers.

Your two volunteers will take it in turns to say a flower name loud enough for everyone to hear. As they say each name, your recorder will write the answer on a board (either a flipchart, visible to the congregation, or a clipboard that only the recorder can see). The volunteers will continue to give alternate answers until one of them fails to give the correct name of a flower or repeats one already given. (You can give them one chance if they repeat too quickly.)

You may like to divide the congregation into two teams so that they can shout out answers to their representatives when they get stuck.

Congratulate the two volunteers on the number of flowers they have named and ask them to return to their seats. Show another of your flowers to the congregation and ask if anyone can name it. Ask a child to come forward to hold the flower. Repeat with each different flower. As you do this, comment on each one, maybe about the beautiful smell, the intricate details of the petals or the soft feel.

Read Genesis 1:11: 'Then God said, "Let the land produce vegetation: seed-bearing plants and trees... according to their various kinds."' Point out that God didn't just make one flower or one type of tree; he made hundreds and hundreds of different flowers. What an amazing creation! (You may like to ask the children to give their flowers to a friend or someone special on the way back to their places. If it is someone's birthday, you may like to collect the flowers into a bouquet and give them to that person as the congregation sings 'Happy birthday'.)

Ask for five volunteer children to come to the front, show each one a card with an animal on it, and ask them to do an impression of that animal for the rest of the congregation to guess. Use picture cards if young children are taking part, and help them to do the impression if necessary.

Show the pictures or models of animals and ask the children to name them and hold them for you.

Read Genesis 1:24: 'And God said, "Let the land produce living creatures according to their kinds; the livestock, the creatures that move along the ground and the wild animals, each according to its kind."'

Again, point out that God didn't just make one animal; he made hundreds and hundreds of different animals. What an amazing creation!

Ask for four volunteers to come forward. Choose people of different ages and sizes, and point out how different they are in height, hair colour, clothing, and so on. Ask the congregation to look round at the people sitting close to them and notice the amazing variety. Just as God made plants and birds and animals according to their kind—each one different, each one amazing, each one special—so he made each of us according to our own individual kind. Each one is different, each one amazing and each one very special. Sometimes we don't like what we look like and sometimes we wish we had different skills and talents. However, God made us as we are. He didn't make a mistake and we are all equally part of his wonderful creation.

Challenge

Challenge the children to go home, look in the mirror and, as they do so, to remember that God made them as they are and thank him for that. Ask the rest of the congregation to take a few moments this week to look in the mirror. Encourage them to read Ephesians 2:10: 'For we are God's handiwork, created in Christ Jesus to do good works, which God prepared in advance for us to do.'

Week 35

YOU ARE SPECIAL

Aim
To demonstrate that each person is special to God

Bible links

- Deuteronomy 7:6 (Treasured possession)
- Isaiah 43:4 (Precious and loved)
- 1 Corinthians 12:12–31 (Different abilities)

You will need

- A variety of teddy bears of different shapes and sizes
- Chairs for the teddies to sit on

The talk works best if you or someone else in the congregation has a collection of teddies and can tell a little story about why each one is so special. Alternatively, the week before this talk, you may want to invite everyone to bring their teddies to church. If you do this, make sure that some people are definitely prepared to say something about why their teddy is special.

Talk outline

Ask the congregation to raise their hands if they have ever owned a teddy bear. Ask how many still have a teddy bear today.

Say that you have brought some of your teddies to church and you would like to introduce them to everybody. Alternatively, say that someone else is going to introduce their special teddy collection, or invite the prearranged members of the congregation to come forward and introduce their teddies one at a time.

For each teddy, explain where the teddy came from and why it is special. For example: 'This teddy is called Barney. He is very special to me because I was given him by my grandad when I was a tiny baby. Barney is actually the same age as me, which is very old for a teddy' or, 'This teddy was given to me on my wedding day. Can you see that it has a little wedding dress on? It reminds me of a very happy day' or, 'This is my favourite of all the teddies because it is so tiny. It is the smallest one in the whole collection and I love the way it sits in the palm of my hand.'

Ask the volunteers to leave their teddies at the front and sit each one on a chair (they can share if necessary). Carefully pick up each teddy in turn and ask if anyone can remember why it is special to its owner. Each teddy will be special for a different reason. If all the teddies were exactly the same as one another, they really wouldn't be special at all. It is their differences that make them extra-special.

In the same way, each one of us is special because we are all so different. God didn't make us all the same; he made us look different, he made us with different temperaments and he gave us all different gifts and abilities. However, one thing is absolutely the same for all of us. Ask the children to listen carefully as you read out two verses from the Bible. Ask them to spot what it is that is the same for each of us.

Read Deuteronomy 7:6, emphasising the last three words: 'The Lord your God has chosen you out of all the peoples on the face of the earth to be his people, *his treasured possession*.'

Read Isaiah 43:4, emphasising the words 'precious' and 'I love you': 'Since you are *precious* and honoured in my sight and because *I love you*.'

If the children don't pick up the words 'treasured possession', 'precious' and 'I love you', repeat the verses with more emphasis.

Just as the teddies are special to their owners because they are all different, in God's eyes we are all precious because we are unique. Emphasise how wonderful it is that God sees us as precious and treasured people.

Point out that some of the teddies are small, some big, some old and some new. There are little defects on some of the teddies—not all of them look perfect—but that does not stop them being loved. In the same way, in God's eyes, age, size and abilities have nothing to do with how precious we are to him. He counts all his children as 'treasured'.

Challenge

Challenge the congregation to find something at home that is 'treasured' by them. This doesn't need to be a cuddly toy; it could be any item that is special to them. Invite them to place it by their bed during the coming week so that they will see it when they get up each day. Ask them to look at it each morning and to remember that, in God's eyes, they are a precious treasure.

Week 36

WHICH IS BIGGER?

Aim
To illustrate that the attitude of our hearts is more important to God than the amount that we give

Bible links

- 2 Corinthians 9:7 (Cheerful giving)
- Acts 20:35 (Better to give than to receive)
- John 3:16 (God gave his Son)
- Mark 12:41–42; Luke 21:1–4 (A widow's offering)

You will need

- The words 'smaller' and 'bigger' written on large pieces of paper
- Pairs of 'smaller' and 'bigger' objects (for example, large and small balls, toy cars, shoes, coats and chocolate bars)
- Pairs of objects with smaller and bigger values (for example, a toy ring and a real ring)

- Two small coins and a £20 note (or a larger amount)
- Tray or table and cloth
- Pieces of card and pens
- A picture of a happy face and a picture of a sad face

Before the talk, lay out your big and small objects (including the money) on the tray or table and cover them with the cloth.

Talk outline

Ask for two child volunteers. If possible, choose someone big and someone small. Ask the taller person to hold the banner with 'bigger' written on it and the shorter person to hold the banner with 'smaller' written on it.

Remove the cover from your objects and explain that you want children to come forward and pick two items that are essentially the same but different sizes. Ask the first volunteer to select an item, then find the comparable item and place each one under the correct banner. If the objects are simply different sizes, this will be straightforward. If the objects are similar but don't vary much in size, encourage the children to think of how one of the objects could be considered 'bigger' than the other. For example, the toy ring and the real ring may be the same size but the real ring will have a much bigger value than the toy ring. The £20 note, too, has a bigger face value than the two small coins.

Ask the children if they can think of any 'big' or 'small' suggestions that can be written on the pieces of card and placed under the correct banners. Encourage the children to include some expensive/inexpensive items.

Once all the objects have been placed under the banners, say that although all the items seem to have been sorted correctly, a story in the Bible would suggest that one pair is incorrect.

Retell the story of the widow's offering, found in Mark 12:41–42 and Luke 21:1–4. Jesus was in Jerusalem with his disciples for the Passover festival. There were crowds of people placing their money into the collection box in the temple court. As Jesus and his friends watched, they saw many rich people giving large amounts of money. (Move to the 'bigger' pile, pick up the £20 note and show it to the congregation.)

Continue with the story, saying that a poor widow walked over to the collection box and placed two small coins in the box. (Move to the 'smaller' pile, pick up the coins and show them to the congregation.)

Jesus told his disciples that, surprisingly, the widow had given far more than all the rich people had done.

Ask the children if they understand how the two small coins could be more than the large amount of money. Explain that Jesus went on to say that the rich people had given only a small part of all the money that they had, but the widow had given everything she had. Some gave out of wealth but she gave out of poverty.

Explain that the same is true for us today. God knows that some people are rich and can give lots of money to the church or to help other people. Others, who have less money, cannot give as much. What is important is the attitude behind the giving. The widow gave because she loved God and wanted to give him everything. The rich were more concerned with looking good in front of other people.

Read 2 Corinthians 9:7: 'Each of you should give what you have decided in your heart to give, not reluctantly or under compulsion, for God loves a cheerful giver.'

Show the happy and sad faces. Explain that all of us have things we can give to God. Some of us don't have much money, but we all have something. God loves us to give our money, talents, time and energy to him cheerfully. He doesn't want us to do this because we feel obliged to do so, but because we love him and want to give him our best.

Challenge

Challenge the congregation to think about how they use their gifts, financial or otherwise. (You may want to use this talk as part of a series about giving.) Remind everyone that, as it says in James 1:17, 'Every good and perfect gift is from above, coming down from the Father of the heavenly lights.'

Week 37

EVERYBODY NEEDED

Aim

To illustrate that everyone in the church
has an important role to play: if someone is
missing, the family is incomplete

Bible links

- 1 Corinthians 12:12–31 (The church as one body)

You will need

- 26 cards with a different letter of the alphabet written
  on each card
- A volunteer to read 1 Corinthians 12:14 and 27

Before the service, hide the cards around the church in very
obvious places. Give the letters 'I' and 'U' secretly to two
members of the congregation. They must not be available for
finding until halfway through the talk.

Talk outline

Explain that you need some help before you can carry out the all-age talk today. You have lost all the cards you need as part of the talk and they seem to have been scattered all around the church. Ask the children to help you find the cards. If there are lots of children present, you may want to limit them to finding one card each. If there are only a few children, they can find as many as they want, but they will need to give the extra cards to someone else in the room (child or adult), keeping just one for themselves.

Eventually there should be a line of volunteers at the front, holding one card each. Make sure you have 24 people. (If the congregation is too small to do this, the cards can be placed on the floor at the front of the church. The children will remain at the front while you explain what to do.)

Ask the children if they know what the letters show. If they don't recognise that it is the alphabet, ask the congregation. Someone will say 'the letters of the alphabet', at which point you should ask the card holders to move themselves into alphabetical order. They may need a bit of help doing this. Try not to make it obvious that two letters are missing.

Once all the letters are in order, ask everyone to say the alphabet while looking at the cards. Don't pause at the place where the letters are missing: you will be surprised how few people notice that any are missing. Ask if anyone has seen a problem. If no one has noticed, say the alphabet slowly, pointing at the letters as you speak. Eventually someone will realise that two letters are missing. Look concerned and say, 'Oh yes, "I" is missing and "U" is missing.' Ask if anyone has seen them. At this point, the two members of the congregation with the hidden letters should raise their hands and a child should go and collect them.

Hold up the two letters and point out that the alphabet will never be complete if 'U' and 'I' are missing. In just the same way, the church will never be complete if 'you' or 'I' are missing.

In Paul's letter to the church in Corinth, he says the church is like a body. Ask someone to read 1 Corinthians 12:14 and 27: 'And so the body is not made up of one part but of many... Now you are the body of Christ, and each one of you is a part of it.'

The passage goes on to talk about the importance of each part of our own bodies. It points out that just as we need every bit of our body, so too we need every person in this church. It doesn't matter whether people are young or old, clever or not so clever, male or female. All of us are absolutely essential in the church.

Just as the alphabet is not complete if some letters are missing, so the church is not complete unless 'You' (pick up the letter 'U') and 'I' (pick up the letter 'I') are part of it.

Challenge

Ask those holding the letters to take them home with them and place them by their beds. Suggest that each morning, when they get up, they look at the letter to remind themselves that they are an essential part of the church. Alternatively, you could have some small pieces of cards and pens at the front and ask each child to write their initials on the card to place by their beds.

Week 38

HOW BIG?

Aim

To illustrate the enormity of God's love for us

Bible links

- Romans 5:8; John 3:16; 15:13; 1 John 4:10 (God's love)
- Ephesians 3:17–19; Psalm 103:11–12 (Height, depth and breadth of love)

You will need

- Tape measure and stopwatch (mobile phone stopwatch is fine); a selection from bathroom scales, barometer, kitchen scales, ruler, measuring spoons
- A globe (or football)
- The following figures written on cards: 237,674 miles (382,500 km); 24,901 miles (40,075 km); 2.9 billion miles (4.7 billion km)
- A volunteer to read Psalm 103:11
- Picture of the solar system (optional)

Talk outline

Hold up each piece of measuring equipment in turn and ask the children if they know what each one can be used for. You may wish to invite volunteers to use each piece—for example, to stand on the bathroom scales (be tactful about who you ask), read out the information on the barometer or weigh an object on the kitchen scales.

Ask the children what all these pieces of equipment have in common. Agree that they all measure things and then ask for a volunteer who is feeling fit and healthy today. Use the stopwatch to time this volunteer carrying out an activity such as jumping up the aisle and back again, or completing 20 star jumps.

Ask for two volunteers who think they could measure (for example) the length of the aisle. While these volunteers carry out the measurement, point out that while all the equipment can be used to make some kind of measurement, only the ruler and tape measure can be used to measure length.

Ask for a volunteer to hold up the card showing the number 237,674 miles (382,500 km). Read the number a few times and ask if anyone can guess what measurement this card could be showing. Explain that it shows the average distance of the moon from the earth (it's an average figure because the moon orbits the earth in an elliptical orbit).

Ask a volunteer to show the card with the number 24,901 miles (40,075 km) on it. Ask if anyone can guess what this number refers to. Explain that it is the circumference round the earth at the equator. If a globe is available, show where the equator is positioned and point out what a long way it is around the whole of the earth. Point out how small your own town, city or village is compared to the whole world. If a globe is not available, use a football in a similar way.

Ask a volunteer to hold up the final card, showing the figure 2.9 billion miles (4.7 billion km). If possible, show a picture of the solar system, pointing out that Neptune is the furthest known planet from the earth. (Pluto is now classed as a dwarf planet and not a true planet.) Say that these numbers are almost beyond our comprehension. They are massive.

Ask your prearranged volunteer to read Psalm 103:11–12: 'For as high as the heavens are above the earth, so great is his love for those who fear him; as far as the east is from the west, so far has he removed our transgressions from us.'

Repeat the first part of this verse. Point out that the distances in space are too huge for us to grasp fully. We can't comprehend even the distance to the furthest planet, and astronomers tell us that there are huge expanses of space stretching far beyond what we currently know. Yet here in this Bible verse we read of something that stretches even higher than the heavens—the love of God. Point out how amazing it is that God's love is far bigger than any distances in space; it is so big that no measure can ever be placed on it.

These verses were written many years before Jesus came into the world. However, in his letter to the Ephesians, the apostle Paul wrote down a special prayer that ties in with these verses from Psalm 103.

Slowly read Ephesians 3:17–19: 'I pray that you, being rooted and established in love, may have the power... to grasp how wide and long and high and deep is the love of Christ, and to know this love that surpasses knowledge—that you may be filled to the measure of all the fullness of God.'

Explain that this is your prayer for the entire congregation, 'that they may grasp how wide and long and high and deep is the love of Christ' for them.

As you finish, use these verses as your prayer.

Challenge

Challenge the congregation to go outside in the dark at some point this week and look up at the night sky. As they do so, ask them to think about how God's love for them is far greater than all the distances in space. It is beyond comprehension.

Week 39

PUTTING ON YOUR CLOTHES

Aim
To use Colossians 3:12 to explain the way we should live as Christians

Bible links

- Colossians 3:12–14 (Spiritual clothing)
- Galatians 5:22–23 (Fruit of the Spirit)

You will need

- A variety of large-size clothes, each with one of the following words in large letters on the back: compassion, kindness, humility, gentleness, patience, forgiveness and love. 'Love' should be larger and brighter than the other words
- A volunteer to read Colossians 3:12–13

Talk outline

Ask the children if they have any favourite clothes or something that they really like wearing. Ask what they might wear in a variety of situations—for example, at a wedding, outside in the rain, playing sport, and so on.

In biblical times, the clothes that people wore were very different from those we wear today. Ask if anyone can tell you any of the differences. You may like to dress a child in clothes similar to those worn in biblical times (such as a nativity play costume). Explain that the Bible actually tells us some 'clothes' that God wants us to wear. Ask if anyone can imagine what they would be.

Ask for a volunteer and help them to put on the first item of clothing, labelled with the word 'compassion'. Ask if someone can read the word and if anyone can explain what it means. Explain that God wants us to care about the suffering of other people and he wants us to try to help. Repeat this process for the words 'kindness' (being considerate; showing people that we care); 'humility' (not thinking of ourselves as too important but placing other people's needs above our own); 'gentleness' (treating people in a loving manner; not pushing them away); 'patience' (not being quick to react when things happen that we don't like; being calm; thinking before we speak) and 'forgiveness' (not holding grudges against people; not always having to fight our corner and show that we are right).

Ask someone to read Colossians 3:12–13 (but not verse 14): 'Therefore, as God's chosen people, holy and dearly loved, clothe yourselves with compassion, kindness, humility, gentleness and patience. Bear with each other and forgive one another if any of you has a grievance against someone. Forgive as the Lord forgave you.'

Ask the children what would happen if they woke up each morning, sat on their bed and looked at their clothes but never got round to putting them on. Talk about how silly people would look, going to work or school in their pyjamas. Some mornings, when it's cold and you are feeling tired, it is a big effort to get dressed. However, your clothes won't ever simply jump on to your body: you have to make the effort to put them on.

In the same way, we won't naturally be compassionate, kind, humble, gentle, patient and forgiving; we need to make the effort to 'put these things on' every day. We need to ask God to help us to have these attitudes and to behave in these ways. We then need to think about them during the day and try to put them into practice.

So far, you have read Colossians 3:12 and 13. Now reread these verses but continue to verse 14: 'And over all these virtues put on love, which binds them all together in perfect unity.' Help a child put on the item of clothing labelled 'love'.

Explain that none of the things you have talked about will have an effect on people around us unless they can see that we love them. It is love that will make us compassionate, kind, humble, gentle, patient and forgiving. God wants us to put on all these things, but, above all, he simply wants us to love each other and the people we come into contact with every day. As a church, you could organise lots of events and have amazing Sunday morning services, but if people are not welcomed and loved when they come along to the church, they will not want to stay here.

Read out what Jesus said in John 13:34–35: 'A new command I give you: love one another. As I have loved you, so you must love one another. By this everyone will know that you are my disciples, if you love one another.'

Challenge

Challenge the congregation to write out Colossians 3:12–14 when they get home, or have the verses printed ready for distribution. Encourage people to place the words in a position where they will see them every day—for example, by their bed, on a kitchen cupboard or in the car. Challenge them to take a few moments each day this week to 'put on' these things and ask God to help them to act in the way the verses suggest.

Week 40

GOD'S LETTER

Aim
To illustrate that the Bible is God's special letter written to us. This theme could tie in with Bible Sunday

Bible links

- John 20:31; 1 John 2:1, 26; 1 Timothy 3:14 ('I write these things')
- 2 Timothy 3:16 (Scripture breathed by God)

You will need

- A variety of cards and letters sealed in envelopes (for example, birthday card, get well card, Valentine's card, electricity bill, dentist's appointment)

Address each card to yourself at the place where your service is being held. You may want to write the cards to yourself as well.

Talk outline

Announce that the postman has been extremely busy this morning as he has delivered lots of post. Because you have a busy day ahead, you wonder whether a few of the children could help you open the letters and sort them out.

Invite children to come forward one at a time to open a letter. After each opening, make a comment about the letter and ask the children to place it somewhere appropriate. For example, say, 'Oh, this is a birthday card from Great-Auntie Mary. She always remembers to send me a card. I think I was always one of her favourites. She's getting a bit forgetful now, though—this card's six months early! Anyway, it's always nice to get a card. Will you put it on the table over there so that everyone can see it?' or 'Oh dear, another bill from the electricity company. The prices just keep going up and up!'

Once all the letters have been opened, pick up each one in turn and have a discussion with yourself about it. For example, pick up the birthday card and say, 'I wonder why Auntie Mary sent me this card. Maybe it's because she knew I'd like this picture on the front. Or maybe she just wanted me to know that she cared about me.'

Pick up the dentist's appointment and say, 'Well, I don't really like going to the dentist very much, so I'm glad they send out appointments or I'd probably never get round to doing it. Then I would get toothache and it would be horrible!'

Pick up the Valentine's Day card and say, 'I used to think buying cards like this was a waste of money, but actually I secretly like getting a card that tells me somebody loves me!'

Explain that letters have many different functions. Some are to warn us about something, such as the need to go to the dentist or pay a bill. Some are to inform us of something, like a postcard telling us that a friend is having a good holiday. Some might be to show us that someone cares, such as a birthday or Christmas card. Some might simply say, 'I love you.'

The Bible is God's letter to us. In the Bible, God sometimes warns us about things, sometimes helps us understand things, sometimes gives us information and sometimes simply shows that he loves us.

God used people to write down the things he wanted us to know, which are now recorded in our Bibles. 2 Timothy 3:16 says that the Bible is 'God-breathed': God speaks to us through the Bible.

There are many people's words recorded in the Bible. The first four books of the New Testament (the Gospels) were written by people called Matthew, Mark, Luke and John. They wrote all about Jesus' life while he was on earth. They recorded the amazing miracles that Jesus carried out and the stories and parables he told. In John 20:31, the disciple called John explains why he thought it was important to write down the words of his Gospel.

Ask someone to read John 20:31: 'But these are written that you may believe that Jesus is the Messiah, the Son of God, and that by believing you may have life in his name.'

Although these words were written many years ago, they still have the same function today—to tell us all about Jesus so that we can get to know him and he can become our friend.

Challenge

Remind the congregation about the cards that show that somebody cares for us. Point out that we shouldn't only tell someone that we care about them on Valentine's Day or birthdays. Challenge everyone to send a card to someone this week that simply tells them they are important and wanted. Challenge everyone to take time to read God's love letter to them—the Bible.

ACTION REQUIRED

Aim
To illustrate that faith without actions is dead.

Bible links

- James 2:14–17 (Faith without works)
- Galatians 6:9 (Don't grow weary)
- Colossians 3:17 (Do all things for God)
- Matthew 25:34–40 ('I was hungry')

You will need

- First aid kit
- Umbrella; water pistol (optional)
- Large bar of chocolate
- Glass of water

You may like to arrange for the four roles to be acted out by one or more actors. (1) Someone pretends they are hurt, so that the first aid kit can be used. (2) Someone squirts the speaker or children with a water pistol, so the umbrella is used. (3) Someone comes to the front pretending to be hungry, and is given the chocolate. (4) Someone pretends to be thirsty after running, so they receive a glass of water.

Talk outline

If possible, invite the children to come to the front so that they can clearly see the items you want to show them. Show the congregation the first aid kit, taking out each item and asking what it would be used for. If someone was injured, the first aid kit could be used to help them. If someone is available to act out the role of an injured person, use the contents of your bag to treat them. For example, if the actor pretends they have broken their arm, you apply a sling.

Show the umbrella and ask what it would be used for. If someone is available to squirt a water pistol, use the umbrella to protect the children. Explain that an umbrella is used to protect someone from the rain.

Show the congregation the large bar of chocolate and ask what it could be used for. People may suggest that it could be for a present or prize, but you are looking for the answer that it could be eaten by someone who was feeling hungry. If an actor is available, they should come to the front and tell you that they are hungry. You should look at your chocolate and then turn aside and put the chocolate away in your pocket or under your Bible.

Show the congregation the glass of water and ask what it could be used for. If available, an actor should run to the front, explaining that they've been out running and really need a drink. You could point out that they could go and get one from somewhere else because you will need the water in the glass for a drink when you've finished the talk.

Quickly remind the congregation that the first aid kit could be used for someone who needs medical help; the umbrella could be used to give protection; the chocolate could provide food (or at least a quick snack), and the glass of water could take away thirst.

Now ask the children what would happen to the injured person if no one picked up the first aid kit and used it to help. The person could be left in a lot of pain.

Ask the children what would happen if someone went outside carrying an umbrella but, when a bad storm developed and the rain poured down, they just kept the umbrella folded up by their side.

Ask what would happen if someone was hungry and saw the chocolate but just looked at it without picking it up and undoing the wrapper.

Ask what would happen if someone was thirsty but they just looked at the water and didn't drink it.

Explain that these illustrations teach us something extremely important on a much bigger scale. In the world today, many people are sick with illnesses that could be prevented. Many people are hungry and desperate for food. Many people have no clean water. Many people are struck by terrible disasters in which storms, earthquakes or floods take away their homes and possessions. Point out that we have a choice. We can see all these things and do nothing about it, or we can take action.

Read Matthew 25:34–40. Explain that Jesus' words in verse 40 are very important. 'Truly I tell you, whatever you did for one of the least of these brothers and sisters of mine, you did for me.' When we see suffering in the world and help someone, even in a small way, we are doing it for Jesus.

It is lovely to sit in church and enjoy hearing about the Bible, sing songs and meet our friends. It is great to be Christians and want to follow God. However, the apostle James says something important in his letter: 'Faith by itself, if it is not accompanied by action, is dead' (James 2:17). We choose whether or not to put our faith into action.

Challenge

Challenge the congregation to think about how they put their faith into action. You may want to use this talk to highlight a project to help people in a particular area of the world.

Week 42

YOU ARE WONDERFUL

Aim
To emphasise that God has made many wonderful things, but each individual person is special and amazing

Bible links

- Psalm 139:14 (Fearfully and wonderfully made)
- Genesis 1:26 (Made in God's image)
- Genesis 1:31 (Good creation)

You will need

- The words of Psalm 139:14 written in large letters
- Three chairs positioned at the front
- 30 cards, each showing one of the following answers:
  ❖ (Question 1) 5, 10, 15
  ❖ (Question 2) 106, 206, 306
  ❖ (Question 3) 150, 360, 210
  ❖ (Question 4) 20, 200, 2000
  ❖ (Question 5) 27, 33, 54

- ❖ (Question 6) 100 km/hr, 165 km/hr, 200 km/hr
- ❖ (Question 7) fingernails, toenails, acrylic nails
- ❖ (Question 8) 32, 28, 10
- ❖ (Question 9) 5000, 50,000, 100,000
- ❖ (Question 10) ear, nose, little toe
- Three adult volunteers to hold up the answers in the correct order

You may wish to colour-code each set of cards so that it is easier to see at a glance which three answers go together (or write 'Question 1', 'Question 2' and so on, on the backs of the cards).

You could have pictures of some of the 'wonders of the world' displayed on a screen, such as the Egyptian pyramids, Taj Mahal, Grand Canyon and Victoria Falls. It is a good idea to have both man-made and natural examples. Members of the congregation may have recently been to visit these places. If possible, use one of their photographs displayed on the screen and ask them a question about it during the talk.

Talk outline

Ask the children what is the most amazing thing they have ever seen, and why they thought it was so great. Open the question up to the rest of the congregation. Show the children some pictures of amazing sights from around the world, if available.

Read out Psalm 139:14: 'I praise you because I am fearfully and wonderfully made.' Although the things that the congregation have described and the pictures that have been shown are amazing, the Bible says that each one of us has been made in an amazing and wonderful way. Ask the congregation if they think that they are amazing (you are likely to get little response). Explain that they are going to take part in a quiz that will show them how amazing they actually are.

Invite the three volunteers to come forward and give each of them their ten answer cards. Ask the first to sit on one of the chairs at the front. Ask the second to sit down but put both hands high up in the air. Ask the third to stand up in front of the third chair.

Explain that you are going to ask a question and each of your three volunteers is going to hold up one possible answer. If the congregation think the sitting volunteer is holding the correct answer, you want them to remain seated. If they think the second volunteer is holding the correct answer, you want them to raise both hands clearly in the air on your signal. If they think the third volunteer is holding the correct answer, you want them to stand up on your signal. Point out that this is all for fun and it doesn't matter if people get the answers wrong.

Read out the first question and all three possible answers (as below). As you read the answers, Volunteer 1 should hold their answer card in front of them, Volunteer 2 should hold the answer card high above their head, and Volunteer 3 should stand up, holding their card. Give the congregation a few seconds to decide on their answer, then count '3, 2, 1' and ask everyone to stay seated, raise their hands or stand, according to the answer they think is correct.

Tell the congregation which is the correct answer (the

ones printed in bold below) and ask everyone to be seated again. Repeat for all ten questions.

1. On average, how many times does a person blink per minute? 5 **10** 15

2. How many bones are there in the human skeleton? 106 **206** 306

3. On average, how long do eyelashes last before they fall out? **150 days** 360 days 210 days

4. How many frowns does it take to create one wrinkle? 20 200 **2000**

5. How many bones are there in one of your hands? **27** 33 54

6. What is the highest recorded speed of a sneeze? 110 km/hr **165 km/hr** 200 km/hr

7. Which grow faster? **Fingernails** Toenails Acrylic nails

8. How many teeth are there in a full adult set? **32** 28 10

9. How many times does the average human heart beat in one day? 5000 times 50,000 times **100,000 times**

10. Where is the smallest bone in the body found? **Ear** Nose Little toe

Ask the volunteers to return to their places. Read out Psalm 139:14 again: 'I praise you because I am fearfully and wonderfully made.'

Point out that God has made us all amazing. We all look different, we all have different skills and abilities but, no matter who we are, God has made us wonderfully.

Ask everyone to listen very carefully while you read

out something God says about them that is written in the Bible. Read slowly from Isaiah 43:4: 'You are precious and honoured in my sight and I love you.'

Sometimes things go wrong and sometimes we can feel that no one cares for us very much. We need to remember that God made us wonderfully and he calls us precious and will always love us.

Challenge

God showed us how precious we were to him by sending Jesus to the earth. Ask the congregation to think of someone who is precious to them, and challenge them to do something specific this week to show that person how precious they are.

Week 43

HARVEST REMINDERS

Aim
To use harvest produce to help us remember to say thank you to God

Bible links

- Genesis 8:22 (Harvest times will never end)
- Isaiah 40:26 (Lift up your eyes)
- Ecclesiastes 9:10 (Use your hands)
- John 3:16; Romans 5:8; 1 John 3:1 (God's love for us)
- Matthew 22:37 (Our love for God)
- Matthew 22:39 (Our love for others)

You will need

- A non-sprouting potato
- A potato with 'eyes' in it (about to sprout)
- Corn on the cob
- A bunch of five bananas

- A cabbage (you need to be able to point out the 'heart' of the cabbage)
- Prearranged readers for the suggested passages (optional).

Talk outline

Assuming that this talk will be used as part of a harvest celebration, begin by showing the congregation the produce that has been given, thanking them for it and explaining who the food will be given to after the harvest services. Explain that while the food will bring joy when it is given to those in need, it can also be a reminder to us of God's wonderful creation.

If possible, ask the children to come to the front so that they have a clear view of the items you are showing.

Show the non-sprouting potato first. Ask the children what it is, what it can be used for and how it would be grown. Next, show them the potato with 'eyes'. Explain that these eyes will sprout and, if the potato is placed in soil, the shoots will eventually develop into new potato plants. The eyes in the potato remind us of our own eyes. At harvest, we take the time to consider the wonder of God's creation. We look at the beauty around us and thank him for the food that we have each day. Near the start of Genesis in the Bible, God speaks to Noah and says, 'As long as the earth endures, seedtime and harvest, cold and heat, summer and winter, day and night will never cease' (Genesis 8:22).

Read Isaiah 40:26: 'Lift up your eyes and look to the heavens: who created all these? He who brings out the starry host one by one, and calls forth each of them by name, because of his great power and mighty strength. Not one of them is missing.'

Too often, we get so involved with other things that we stop looking at the beauty around us. Encourage people to take the time to look during this harvest time.

Show everyone the corn on the cob. Ask the children what it is, what it can be used for and how it would be grown. Explain that corn in this form is often described as an 'ear' of corn. At harvest, this can remind us of our own ears and all the amazing things we can hear in the world. Ask the children if they have any favourite sounds. Suggest that, later in the day, people could go and stand outside for a few moments and listen to all the sounds around them. They could then thank God for each sound that they hear.

Show everyone the bunch of bananas. Ask the children what they are, what they can be used for and how they would be grown. Ask if they can guess what part of the body you are going to say they remind you of. (Point out that there are five of them.) Explain that the five bananas remind you of a hand; in fact, the real name for a cluster of bananas is 'a hand'. At harvest time, these bananas remind us of the amazing things we can do with our hands and the rest of our bodies. Too often, we take for granted our ability to move, pick things up and feel things. At harvest it is good to stop and thank God for all these things. The hand of bananas can also remind us of the way God wants us to use our hands for him. Ecclesiastes 9:10 says, 'Whatever your hand finds to do, do it with all your might.'

Show the congregation the cabbage. Ask the children

what it is, what it can be used for and how it would be grown. Ask the congregation if anyone can predict what part of the body the cabbage could help us think about.

Explain that the inside of the cabbage is called the 'heart'. This can remind us of three things at harvest. Firstly, as the heart is often the symbol for love, it reminds us of the amazing love that God has for us (John 3:16; Romans 5:8; 1 John 3:1). Secondly, it reminds us that God wants us to love him with all our hearts (Matthew 22:37). Thirdly, it reminds us that God wants us to love other people (Matthew 22:39). Read whichever of the above verses you feel would be appropriate.

Challenge

Challenge the congregation to go out for a walk in a park or in the countryside, if possible. Ask them to stop at some point and use the senses you have thought about today. Ask them to look around, listen to the sounds and thank God for the way he loves them.

Week 44

WHO WILL YOU CALL?

Aim
To illustrate that we can call upon God at any time, in any place

Bible links

- Jeremiah 29:12–13; Psalm 18:6 (God hears)
- Psalm 120:1 (God answers)
- Psalm 50:15 (God rescues)
- Psalm 91:15; Psalm 145:18 (God is close in times of trouble)

You will need

- Various communication devices (mobile phone, landline phone, old-fashioned phone, walkie-talkie)
- A few well-known telephone numbers written on large pieces of paper or displayed on the screen (for example, emergency services 999; directory enquiries 118 118; Childline 0800 1111; local radio station or sports centre; church phone number, and so on)

- Prearranged readers for Jeremiah 29:12–13; Psalm 120:1; Psalm 50:15 and Psalm 145:18

The phone numbers should be of varying difficulty so that they can be guessed by different age groups.

Talk outline

Show the congregation the communication devices one at a time, commenting on their use in different situations. Sometimes it can be inconvenient to receive a phone call—for example, at meal times, when you are in the middle of doing something important or too late at night. Despite this, most of us would not want to be without a phone. Before mobile phones were invented, it was much more difficult to keep in touch with people. Now, many people will not leave home without a mobile.

Most people have 'favourite' numbers on their phone. Some phone companies even allow them to be free call numbers. These favourite numbers are for the people we ring most often, usually a child, spouse, close relative or close friend. Sometimes we know these numbers off by heart.

Say that you are going to show some famous numbers that people often know by heart. Start by showing 999. Ask the children if they know what will happen if they call that number. Some of the children may know what happens when someone answers the call, but be ready to explain that the operator will ask a few questions and decide which of the emergency services are needed. The operator will then send the necessary help to the location given. Emphasise the importance of not calling this number unless there is an emergency.

Show 118 118 and see if anyone knows what would happen if this number was called. Discuss how directory enquiries works and its uses.

Repeat with each of the telephone numbers. As the numbers become more difficult, you may want to have clues ready, in case no one guesses them correctly. For example, if the local school number is used, you might say, 'This number would be called if one of the children were sick on a weekday' or 'If I wanted to speak to [insert the local head teacher's name] I could call this number.'

The Bible often talks about calling God. Show the different phones again and ask the children how we would call God. Ask the prearranged readers to read the following verses and, after each is read, comment on the meaning.

- Jeremiah 29:12–13: 'Then you will call on me and come and pray to me, and I will listen to you. You will seek me and find me when you seek me with all your heart.' God will always listen when we call on him.

- Psalm 120:1: 'I call on the Lord in my distress and he answers me.' When we are sad and things have gone wrong, we can call out to God and he will always listen and answer.

- Psalm 50:15: 'Call on me in the day of trouble; I will deliver you.' When we are in trouble, we can call out to God and he will help us through every situation we find ourselves in.

- Psalm 145:18: 'The Lord is near to all who call on him, to all who call on him in truth.' Whenever we call out to God, he is always near to us.

Remind the congregation that although it is sometimes inconvenient for us to answer the telephone and sometimes we may not feel like talking, this is never true of God. He is always there when we call to him. He will always listen and will always be pleased to hear from us.

Challenge

Ask the congregation to think about phone calls that have made them happy. Remind them that although it is good to call on God in times of trouble, it is also good to call on him when things are going well. Challenge the congregation to spend a few moments each day this week 'calling on God' as soon as they wake up in the morning.

Week 45

LIVING STONES

Aim
To illustrate that the church is more than a building; it is made up of people. This talk ties in well with All Saints Day

Bible links

- 1 Peter 2:5 (Being built into a house)
- Matthew 16:18 (Peter the rock)
- Acts 20:28 (Church of God)
- Acts 5:42; Hebrews 10:25 (Meeting together)
- Ephesians 1:22–23 (The body of Christ)

You will need

- Large cardboard boxes
- Paper; masking tape; black marker pen
- Photos or pictures of congregation members
- Pictures of various churches displayed on the screen, including recognisable local buildings (optional)

During the talk, the cardboard boxes will be built into a church. In preparation, set up the boxes into a church shape and draw on some features in thick black lines. These lines should run across adjacent boxes so that they can be used to guide the children as they put the church together. The features needn't be complicated—just double doors and a couple of windows.

On the back of each box, stick a picture of a person. If possible, the pictures should be of people in your congregation. Stick a piece of paper over each picture with masking tape, so that it can be easily removed during the talk. (Tape all the edges of the paper so that, even if the box is turned upside-down, the picture will still not be revealed.) You may wish to add a box in the shape of a tower or steeple to create a traditional church shape.

If possible, keep the boxes out of sight until they are needed.

Talk outline

Explain that you need to carry out some building work this morning and will need some help. Ask for volunteers to carry the boxes to the front of the room and place them in a pile. Ask if any of the children are good at building things. Say that you want to build a church and ask a few of them to come forward to help. Show the children the black outlines of doors and windows and ask them to use the lines as a guide to building the church.

Allow the children time to build, giving a commentary as they do so—for example, 'Yes, a church needs big doors so that lots of people can get in if they arrive at the same time' or, 'I just drew the windows with plain glass, although lots of churches have stained glass windows', and so on.

Once the church has been built, ask the children if they can see any differences between the 'box church' they have just built and their own church building.

Show the pictures of different churches, if available, pointing out distinguishing features. Explain that when people think about churches, they usually think about the building; however, in the Bible, the church is not a building.

Read Matthew 16:18: 'You are Peter, and on this rock I will build my church.' Jesus wasn't going to build a church on top of Peter, or he would have been squashed! Jesus meant that he was going to use Peter as a key leader in the church.

Ask for some more volunteers to come forward. Show these volunteers how to turn a brick around and remove the piece of paper, revealing the picture beneath. As each picture is revealed, comment on the person shown. For example, say, 'Oh, look who we have here! Mrs Jones, what are you doing on the back of a church brick?' or 'And here we have James! So we've got pictures of older people and children and babies' and so on.

Read 1 Peter 2:5: 'You also, like living stones, are being built into a spiritual house.' Explain that the true meaning of the word 'church' is not the building but the people within it. The Greek word for church is 'ekklesia', which is formed from two words meaning 'assembly' and 'to call out'. So 'church' means people called by God to form a group together. In the Bible, this group of people is sometimes described as the body of Christ.

Read Ephesians 1:22–23: 'And God placed all things under [Jesus'] feet and appointed him to be head over everything for the church, which is his body, the fullness of him who fills everything in every way.'

As members of the church, we need to look after one another, just as we look after our physical bodies.

Challenge

In the book of Acts we read about the start of the church—when followers of Jesus began meeting together. Ask the congregation to close their eyes and listen carefully as you read out some verses about the early church. Challenge them to think about their part in being the church today.

Read Acts 2:42–47. Pause and mention a few of the qualities in the passage. Challenge the congregation to think about how well the church of today is functioning. Are we 'devoted to one another'? Are people filled with awe at what we do? Would we be described as 'together', either as a local church or a wider church?

Week 46

SPEAKING FLOWERS

Aim
To aid the understanding of Remembrance Day by looking at the significance of flowers when showing love

Bible links

- Matthew 6:28–30 (God clothes the flowers)
- Matthew 6:25, 34 (Do not worry)
- John 15:13 (Jesus gives his life)
- John 8:36 (Jesus gives freedom)

You will need

- A red rose
- A large daisy from a florist shop, or a paper daisy (yellow circle with white removable petals).
- Display board for the paper daisy (optional)
- Mistletoe, or a picture of mistletoe
- A red poppy (real, if possible, or an artificial Remembrance Day poppy)

- Someone to read John McCrae's poem 'In Flanders Fields' (optional)

Talk outline

Explain that recently you have been thinking about flowers. You may want to tell a story about why you recently bought some.

Ask the children if they have ever bought flowers for someone or if they know anyone who has. Ask why they might buy someone flowers. Explain that most flowers are bought to say 'thank you', to show someone you care, to say 'I love you' or simply because they look nice. When someone buys flowers, they will usually choose the flowers that either they or the recipient likes best. However, certain flowers traditionally have a specific meaning.

Show the congregation the red rose and ask if anyone knows when this flower is traditionally bought. Explain that the majority of red roses are bought around 14 February, which is Valentine's Day. It means 'I love you'.

Show the congregation the daisy. Ask if anyone can guess what the daisy traditionally stands for. Explain that it is meant to show 'loyalty in love'—the idea that someone will love the other person for ever. Ask if anyone knows a game that children play using a daisy. Sometimes people pretend that pulling the petals off a daisy can tell you whether someone loves you or not. They pull off one petal and say, 'Loves me'; they pull off the next petal and say, 'Loves me not.' This continues until all the petals have been removed. The phrase that is spoken as the last petal is removed is supposed to show whether the person they are thinking about loves them or not. Demonstrate using your real or paper daisy. Point out that this is just a silly bit of fun.

Show the congregation the mistletoe and ask if anyone knows what it is and what it is traditionally used for. Explain that, at Christmas, mistletoe is traditionally hung above a doorway. Whoever stands under the mistletoe is supposed to receive a kiss.

Show the congregation the poppy and ask if anyone knows anything special about it. Say that it is traditionally used on and around Remembrance Day. There are a few different reasons given for using the poppy in this way, but you are going to tell them one of these reasons. Explain that in World War I, an area of land that spanned Belgium and north-west France was called Flanders, and it was the scene of some of the worst fighting. The area was devastated and ended up as a mudbath, with all natural wildlife destroyed. However, almost as soon as the fighting ceased, poppies began to sprout from the ground, between the rough wooden crosses that had been placed on the soldiers' graves. Poppy seeds, which can lie dormant in the soil for over 80 years, had begun to grow as the soil was disturbed.

In 1915, a Canadian doctor called John McCrae saw the fields covered in poppies and wrote a famous poem called 'In Flanders Fields'. (A prearranged volunteer could read the poem at this point.)

Over time, the poppy has become the symbol of remembrance. We buy poppies to show that we will not forget the many men and women who have laid down their lives for us in the past (and continue to do so) so that we can enjoy the freedom we have today. The money we spend on poppies goes to help the people involved in the armed forces and their families. Point out that many of these people paid the ultimate price for freedom: they gave up their lives.

You may want to tie this in with the life and death of Jesus. Read the words of Jesus in John 15:13: 'Greater love has no one than this: to lay down one's life for one's friends.' Jesus was pointing towards the fact that he would eventually give his own life so that we could be forgiven.

Read John 8:36: 'So if the Son sets you free, you will be free indeed.' Explain that Jesus' death and resurrection brought us freedom.

Challenge

Encourage the congregation to think about the people who have given their lives to bring peace, and to think also about Jesus, who gave his life to bring us peace with God. Challenge them to think what they could do to encourage peace in the world. Do they need to bring peace in a relationship? How can they encourage peace in the home, at school or in the workplace?

Week 47

ALL IN A NAME

Aim

To teach some of the names of God that are used in the Bible

Bible links

- Exodus 3:14 (Yahweh)
- Genesis 17:1 (El Shaddai)
- Psalm 23:1 (Jehovah Raah)
- Genesis 22:14 (Jehovah Jireh)
- Judges 6:24 (Jehovah Shalom)

You will need

- A book of names and their meanings
- The following names written on large cards: Yahweh, El Shaddai, Jehovah, Jehovah Raah, Jehovah Jireh, Jehovah Shalom
- Volunteer parents to explain why they chose their children's names

Talk outline

Ask the children if anyone knows your name. If you are a visiting speaker, you may want to give clues, such as 'It begins with...' Explain that when parents are expecting a baby, they discuss what they are going to call their child. Once a baby is born, people are keen to find out what name has been chosen.

Sometimes people choose a name because they like the sound of it. Sometimes a child is named after a parent or other relative, and sometimes a child is given a name because of its meaning. Invite your prearranged volunteers to explain why they chose particular names for their children.

Show the congregation the book of names. Explain that most people's names have a meaning, and ask if anyone would like to know what their name means. Read out the meanings from the book. If you know the people in the congregation, you may want to choose a few of their names beforehand. This way, you can be certain that some of the definitions you give will be particularly appropriate to the people with those names.

In biblical times, names had far greater importance than they do today. Usually they meant something very specific. Here are some examples:

- Samuel means 'God hears'. Remind the congregation of the story of Hannah crying out to God for a child.

- Moses means 'drawn from the water'. Moses was hidden in the bulrushes at the edge of the River Nile and was drawn out by Pharaoh's daughter.

- Peter means 'a rock'. Jesus changed Simon's name to Peter when he announced that Peter would be the rock on which the church would be built.

In the Bible, many names are used to describe God. Say that you are going to look at a few of them today.

Show the word 'Yahweh'. In the Bible, this word is used for God over 6500 times. It's the name that God used for himself when he first spoke to Moses. It means 'I am', or 'the Lord'—but not 'lord' in the ordinary human sense (lord of the manor, for example). Yahweh is the Lord of lords, the highest Lord, the creator and absolute ruler of all things. There is no one as great as God.

Show the name 'El Shaddai'. This means that God is the almighty God who provides for all our needs. It is used to suggest the way a mother cares for the needs of a child. Although God is far greater than we can ever imagine, he still cares for us and loves us.

Ask for a volunteer to show the words 'Yahweh' and 'El Shaddai' next to each other. Explain that these two names tell us two different things about God. He is greater than everything, but he also cares for us very much.

Show the word 'Jehovah'. Explain that, in some Bibles, this word is used instead of Yahweh, so it too means 'Lord'. The name Jehovah is usually used with another word attached.

Show the examples:

- Jehovah Raah: this means 'the Lord my shepherd'.
- Jehovah Jireh: this means 'the Lord will provide'.
- Jehovah Shalom: this means 'the Lord is peace'.

Explain that the names Yahweh and Jehovah express the greatness of God. El Shaddai and the words added to Jehovah express God's care for us. He is not only the great creator; he also wants to care for us as a shepherd cares for his sheep; he wants to provide for us and bring us peace. Isn't that amazing?

Challenge

Point at each of the cards in turn and read the name of God displayed there. After reading each name, challenge everyone to remember what God is like as they go through different experiences in the coming week.

For example, read the name 'Yahweh' and say, 'God is greater than all things. He is the great creator and he knows everything. Whatever you go through this week, God already knows about it. He has the power to help you through every situation.'

Read the name 'El Shaddai' and say, 'God is great but also loving. He cares for us more than a mother would for her child. There is never a situation where God will not be there to care for you.'

Read the name 'Jehovah Raah' and say, 'The Lord is our shepherd. Isn't it wonderful that, even though God is so great, he cares for us in the same way as a shepherd would look after his sheep? Isn't it amazing that, as in the story of the lost sheep, God will look for us if we wander away from him and will be delighted when we come back to him?'

Week 48

WAITING IS GOOD

Aim
To illustrate the importance of Advent as the Christmas season approaches

Bible links

* Matthew 1—2; Luke 1:26—2:20 (Christmas story)

You will need

* Two football kits
* Two sets of shin pads
* Two pairs of slippers
* Two water bottles
* A picnic rug
* Plastic containers, plates and cups
* Picnic chairs
* A beach bag containing an empty purse and a torn swimming costume/trunks
* Football goalposts (can be made from boxes or chairs)

Talk outline

Ask for two volunteers who would like to play a game of football. (Choose people who will fit into the football kits.) Give them the football kits and shin pads and, as they put on each item, point out how useful that item is for playing football. For example, as they put on the shirts, say that it is important to wear the correct shirts so that everybody knows which team they play for. As the shin pads are put on, say how important it is to protect your legs. Lastly, give the volunteers the slippers. When they object, look surprised and ask what is wrong. If necessary, ask the congregation what is the matter. Say something like, 'Oh well, you'll just have to manage! I forgot that you don't usually play football in slippers.' Then ask one of the volunteers to stand in goal and ask the other to see how many goals they can score.

When the volunteers point out that they haven't got a ball, say something like, 'How disappointing! I suppose we can't play after all. I wish I'd bothered to be better prepared. I never thought about bringing a ball. Oh well, you'd better sit down, then.'

Ask if anyone is hungry and select three volunteers. Explain that they are going to have a picnic with you. Give them the picnic rug to spread out, the chairs to set up and the crockery to place on the rug. Give them the plastic containers and ask them to set out the food because you're really hungry and want to eat straight away. When they point out that there is no food, groan that you really want something to eat. Then say something like, 'Oh well, I suppose we can't have a picnic, then. What's the point of having a picnic without food? I should have been better prepared. Sorry!'

Once they are seated, pick up the beach bag. Say that you might not be able to play football or have a picnic but at least you can tell everybody about the trip to the seaside you're going to go on after the service. (If the weather is bad, joke that there is going to be a heatwave later.) You are really looking forward to having a swim in the sea and you have packed your costume. Pull out the torn costume. Hold it up for everyone to see and express your disappointment that you won't be able to wear it. Say something like, 'Oh well, even if I can't swim or sunbathe, I can at least get a cone of chips or an ice cream from the beach hut.' Pull out your purse, open it and express your disappointment that it is empty.

Explain that whatever we do in our lives, everything needs some preparation. Before we can eat, someone has to cook the food; before we can learn in school, our teachers need to prepare the lessons; before we can play in a football match, someone must organise the game and transport the players to the match. If people don't do any preparation, then things are usually disappointing.

In the lead-up to Christmas, there are many things that need doing. Ask the children what their favourite Christmas preparations are—putting up the tree or the decorations, going to parties, writing cards, visiting Santa, and so on.

Explain that Advent is a time of preparation. Many people have Advent calendars, which they use to build up the excitement as they move towards Christmas Day. Many churches have Advent wreaths, which help us prepare for

Christmas as each candle is lit week by week. The season of Advent doesn't really mean preparation in the sense of buying presents or putting up decorations. It means preparing our hearts for the real message of Christmas.

Remind the congregation how disappointing it was earlier when you weren't properly prepared for the football match, the picnic or the trip to the beach. If you'd stopped to think properly about what you were going to do, you would have been better prepared and you would have enjoyed things much better. In the same way, if we prepare our hearts by thinking about God and the real meaning of Christmas, then when Christmas arrives it will be even better than we imagined.

Challenge

Challenge the children to stop as they open their Advent calendars and think about what a difference the birth of Jesus made to the world. Challenge the congregation to buy an extra Advent calendar which shows the Christmas story and can be opened alongside the chocolate ones, so that families are reminded daily about the true meaning of Christmas.

Week 49

LIGHTING IT UP

Aim

To demonstrate what it means when Jesus says that he is the light of the world and to consider how we also can be lights

Bible links

- John 8:12; 9:5 (Light of the world)
- 1 John 1:5 (God is light)
- 1 John 1:7 (Walk in the light)
- Psalm 119:105 (God's word is light)
- Matthew 5:14, 16 (Let your light shine)
- John 12:35–36 (Light that guides)

You will need

- Two bright torches or flashlights
- A chair and an adult volunteer to stand on it while flashing a light
- A blindfold and an adult volunteer to wear it for an obstacle course

- Cardboard boxes
- Four more chairs; a dark-coloured blanket, duvet cover or throw; another volunteer
- A book

Before the talk, pile some boxes on top of each other at the front, to create an obstacle course. Your blindfold volunteer will need to walk across the front of the room, deliberately bumping into obstacles. This adult needs to act the part well, putting their arms in front of them and walking into the obstacles. Make sure they can either peep under the blindfold or clearly see the direction of the obstacles before you blindfold them.

Also before the talk, place one chair at the front for an adult to stand on. Explain to your volunteer that they will be flashing a torch on and off, as if they are a lighthouse.

Set up another four chairs covered with your dark cloth, to give the impression of a cave. The cave needs to be as dark as possible, so use several covers if necessary. If the covers are still too thin to keep out the light, arrange for your volunteer to act as if it is too dark inside to read from the book.

Talk outline

Show the congregation one of your torches and explain that today you are going to be thinking about light. Ask your first volunteer to come forward, stand on the chair and hold the torch. Ask them to begin flashing the torch on and off, and ask the children to guess what they are pretending to be.

Once the children have guessed correctly, ask them what job a lighthouse does and why it is important that a light should be flashed out to sea. A lighthouse prevents ships from crashing into the rocks. It warns of danger and protects people from danger. Ask the volunteer to remain standing on the chair.

Invite your second volunteer to the front and explain that you are going to blindfold them and ask them to walk from one side of the room to another. You will walk alongside, but you will only intervene if the volunteer is in danger. Lead the blindfolded volunteer to the start position. When you say 'go', this person should walk slowly, as if unsure of their steps, but should deliberately walk into the boxes, causing as much of a commotion as possible. At the other side of the room, remove the blindfold and ask the volunteer why they bumped into so many obstacles. The person should reply that they couldn't see where they were going; it was like trying to find their way around in the dark.

Ask for a brave volunteer who dares to go into the dark cave. Invite someone to the front and ask them to sit inside. Give them a book and ask them to read it to you. Pull the covers down so that no light can get in (or use a prearranged volunteer, as suggested above). When the volunteer has made it clear that they can't read the book because it is too dark, ask them if they want to borrow a torch. Hand your second torch to the person and ask them to read a few of the words; this time they will be able to because of the light. Lift up the cover so that the congregation can see the volunteer.

Explain that, in the Bible, Jesus describes himself as 'the light of the world' (John 8:12; 9:5). This phrase can be difficult to understand, but what we have seen during this talk can help us.

- The lighthouse: The lighthouse shines out a light that warns people of danger and protects them from harm. In the same way, Jesus warns us of dangers that can destroy our lives. He encourages us to live in ways that will keep us safe. When God says that we shouldn't do something (you may want to talk about the ten commandments here), it is not because he wants to spoil our fun; it is because he wants to protect us from danger.

- Finding our way in the dark: Ask the children if they have ever been in a place that is absolutely dark. Ask them to imagine finding their way along a path at night-time with no moonlight or stars or street lamps: they could easily get hurt or lost. When the volunteer was blindfolded, it was like stumbling along a path in the darkness. They couldn't see where they were going, so they crashed into things. On a dark night, a torch illuminates the path so that we can see our way ahead. When Jesus says he is the light of the world, he means that not only does he protect us from danger but he also guides us in the way we should go. In John 12:35, Jesus says, 'Whoever walks in the dark does not know where they are going.' Jesus the light of the world will guide us throughout our lives. Psalm 119:105 says, 'Your word is a lamp for my feet, a light on my path.' One way to find our way through life is to read and listen to God's words. They will lead us and show us the right way to live.

- Inside the cave: Not only does Jesus show us the way
  ahead; he is also present here with us now, being
  the light in our lives today. Sometimes things can go
  wrong and it can seem as if there is darkness around
  us. However, even then Jesus is beside us, bringing us
  comfort and taking away fear.

When Jesus says he is the light of the world, he is saying
that he protects, leads, guides, comforts, takes away fear and
points us towards heaven.

Challenge

Read Matthew 5:14, 16: 'You are the light of the world. A
town built on a hill cannot be hidden… In the same way, let
your light shine before others, that they may see your good
deeds and glorify your Father in heaven.' Point out that Jesus
describes himself as the light of the world but he also uses
the same phrase to describe us. Challenge the congregation
to think about how they can be a light in every place they
find themselves this coming week.

Week 50

GOD'S SURPRISE

Aim
To illustrate that, despite the prophecies about Jesus, God surprised everybody when he sent Jesus as a baby

Bible links

- Matthew 1:18—2:12; Luke 2:1–20 (Christmas story)
- Isaiah 7:14; 9:6–7; Micah 5:2 (Prophecies)

You will need

- A Christmas cracker (or more than one)
- 'Lucky dip' bags
- Christmas stocking (if possible, containing a few cheap presents)

Talk outline

Ask the children if they like surprises. Encourage them to think back to birthdays or to Christmas and think of the biggest surprise they have ever had. Invite a few of them to share it with the congregation. Ask if they have ever had other surprises—unexpected guests, bad news, a surprise holiday. If possible, share with the children a big surprise that you have had.

Show the children the Christmas cracker and ask what they think will be inside. Point out that, although we all know there will probably be a hat and a joke, we don't know what the present will be. Ask for two volunteers (or more if you are using more crackers) to pull the cracker. Let the volunteers look inside, put the hats on and tell the joke. Say that we had some clues about what would be in the crackers, but the actual present was a surprise.

Tell these volunteers to return to their seats and ask for more (the number will depend on how many 'lucky dip' bags you have available).

Ask the children what they think will be in the bags. If someone tries to read the contents list, point out that this only gives a vague idea of what will be inside or it would spoil the surprise. For example, it will say 'sweets' rather than the exact kind of sweets and 'novelty' rather than the actual gift. Ask the children to open the bags to see what is inside.

Show the Christmas stocking and ask if anyone can guess what is inside. Some of their guesses may be correct, but no one really knows what the gifts are, apart from you, the person who put the gift together. Ask for volunteers to come forward to open the presents.

Explain that in the Old Testament God promised that he would send the Messiah. The Jewish people expected the Messiah to be a great king and leader who would rescue them from their suffering. God told various prophets about the coming of the Messiah: he gave hints about the gift he would eventually send. Ask people to read out the following passages before you explain them briefly:

- Isaiah 9:6: 'For to us a child is born, to us a son is given.' The Messiah would arrive as a child.

- Isaiah 9:7: 'He will reign on David's throne and over his kingdom... for ever.' The Messiah would be a relative of King David.

- Isaiah 7:14: 'The virgin will conceive and give birth to a son.' His mother would be a virgin.

- Micah 5:2: 'But you, Bethlehem Ephrathah, though you are small among the clans of Judah, out of you will come for me one who will be ruler over Israel.' The Messiah would be born in Bethlehem.

Explain that there are many more prophecies about Jesus' birth, life, death and resurrection. You might have a list ready for people to take away if they would like to look at the others.

God gave various clues about the gift that he was going to send, but in the end it was a complete surprise. Despite the clues, no one expected Jesus, the promised king, to be born in a poor, dirty place. No one guessed that he would be placed in a manger from which animals ate their food. No one imagined that his first visitors would be poor shepherds.

At Christmas we all receive lots of lovely surprises, but it was God's amazing surprise for us that started it all off—the birth of Jesus.

Challenge

This Christmas, challenge people to remember God's surprise as they open their presents. If you take part in any events where presents are given to those who are less fortunate (shoebox appeals, toy collections, and so on), challenge the congregation to get involved and give someone in need a surprise this Christmas.

Week 51

UNWRAPPING THE STORY

Aim
To look at the true meaning of Christmas

Bible links

- Matthew 1:18—2:12; Luke 2:1–20 (Christmas story)
- John 3:16 (God gave his Son)

You will need

- Four boxes of different sizes, gift-wrapped:
  - ❖ Box 1 contains tinsel or decorations
  - ❖ Box 2 contains three smaller beautifully wrapped parcels
  - ❖ Box 3 contains crackers
  - ❖ Box 4 contains a picture of a winter scene or artificial snow
- A fifth gift-wrapped box, containing something that represents the true meaning of Christmas, such as a nativity scene or a baby doll

The parcels in Box 2 don't need to have anything inside them, although, if the children are going to open them, you may want to include a small gift in each one.

The fifth box is slightly different in that it needs to unfold into a cross shape. Prepare a cardboard box by cutting it apart so that, when it is unwrapped, it will unfold easily.

With the box opened out, write the word GOD'S verti-cally, down the longer part of the cross, and the word SON horizontally, using the 'O' in both words. Put the box back together and hold the sides with small pieces of tape.

This box needs to be carefully wrapped in Christmas paper so that it looks like the other four boxes, but it must be opened last.

If time is limited, just use Boxes 1–3 and then the final box.

Talk outline

Ask the children what they are most looking forward to about Christmas. Ask the rest of the congregation if they have a favourite part of Christmas. Show the first four presents and ask for a volunteer to come forward to open the first one. The order in which the first four parcels are unwrapped is unimportant, but the box revealing the true meaning of Christmas must be left to the end.

As each present is unwrapped, explain how the box contents relate to different aspects of Christmas:

- Tinsel/decorations: For many people, their favourite part of Christmas is putting up the Christmas tree, decorating the house or looking at the Christmas lights that appear in the streets. The lights and decorations are exciting and wonderful to see, but there are more important things.

- Presents: A wonderful part of Christmas is giving and receiving presents. It is so exciting to come downstairs on Christmas morning and see the piles of presents, or to wake up and feel the weight of a full stocking on the end of the bed. However, Christmas is so much more than presents.

- Crackers: Ask for volunteers to come to the front to pull the crackers. Demonstrate how difficult it is to pull a cracker on your own. The crackers remind us that Christmas is a time for families and friends. It is wonderful to have parties and get together with people who are special to us. (You may want to remind people to think about those who are lonely and sad at this time of year and encourage them to include others in their celebrations.)

- Winter scene: Ask who likes the snow. Ask the children what they like to do best when it snows in the winter— making snowmen, snowball fights, sledging, and so on. All these are great fun to do, but there are still more important things about Christmas.

- Fifth box: Show the children the fifth box and carefully remove some of the wrapping so that a child can lift the baby doll or nativity scene out. Ask why there would be a baby in the box. When the answer 'Baby Jesus was born at Christmas' is given, agree with the answer but point out that this box is going to show us that Christmas is about even more than just a baby. Undo the box so that the sides fall down, and hold it up to show the cross shape. Ask a child to read what it says inside, asking them to read the word going downwards first and then the word written across—GOD'S SON.

Many babies are born at Christmas time, but baby Jesus changed the world. Remind the congregation that this baby was God's Son sent from heaven. Explain that he would eventually die so that we could be forgiven for the wrong things we've done, and that he would come back to life again. His life, death and resurrection would change the world for ever.

Jesus was God's gift to all of us. Ask someone to read John 3:16: 'For God so loved the world that he gave his one and only Son, that whoever believes in him shall not perish but have eternal life.'

If time allows, you may want to read Romans 6:23: 'For the wages of sin is death, but the gift of God is eternal life in Christ Jesus our Lord.' Expand on this, pointing out that God's gift is the best gift ever.

Challenge

Challenge the congregation to think about God's gift as they wrap up their presents for other people. You may wish to challenge them to buy a present for someone in need. You may like to have simple crosses available so that the children can write GOD'S SON on them to help them remember.

Week 52

THROW IT AWAY

Aim
To use rubbish to demonstrate the need to get rid of things in our lives that stop us from following God more closely and also hinder other people from seeing him. This can be tied in with the theme of a new year

Bible links

- Ephesians 4:31; Colossians 3:8; 1 Peter 2:1 ('Rid yourselves…')

You will need

- Any kind of (clean) rubbish: plastic bottles, crisp packets, jars, sweet wrappers, and so on

Label each piece of rubbish with one of the following words: lies, stealing, unwholesome talk, bitterness, rage, anger, envy, slander, malice, filthy language, deceit, hypocrisy, gossip. You may want to select words from this list rather than using all of them, depending on the age of the children.

Talk outline

Depending on where the all-age slot occurs within the service, you may want to have the rubbish spread out on the floor before the service begins or have it ready in a clean bin to be emptied out in front of the congregation. It can work well if someone comes to the front and pretends to trip with the bin so that all the rubbish spills out.

Express your disgust at all the rubbish. Make faces and hold your nose, pointing out that you can't believe this beautifully clean building could be covered in horrible rubbish. Ask the children what they think you ought to do about it. Ask if anyone would like to come and collect it up for you. If you don't get any volunteers, choose someone to come and help you. As they pick up one piece of rubbish and move towards the bin, stop them and say something like, 'Hold on a minute, it looks as if there's something attached to that rubbish.' Read out the word on the label.

Look puzzled and pretend to be thinking. Explain that the word reminds you of something but you can't quite remember what. Invite other volunteers to come up to see if there are any words on the other items of rubbish. As each piece of rubbish is examined, read the word and check that the children understand what it means. For example, 'malice' means ill-will against someone, desiring to harm someone; 'unwholesome talk' means unhelpful, harmful, hurtful talk or gossip. Don't place the rubbish in the bin yet.

As the words are read, keep mentioning that they remind you of something. As you get to the end, tell the congregation that you've remembered what all these words remind you of.

Pick up your Bible and explain that in three books of the Bible (Ephesians, Colossians and 1 Peter), the writers speak about getting rid of certain things in our lives, which are like rubbish. Explain that you have combined all the verses together into one, and read them out: 'Therefore rid yourself of lies (falsehood), stop stealing, get rid of bitterness, rage, anger, slander, unwholesome talk, malice, filthy language, deceit, envy, hypocrisy, gossip. Instead be kind and compassionate to one another, forgiving each other, just as in Christ God forgave you.' (You can read all the verses separately if you prefer.)

Explain that God wants us to get rid of all the 'rubbish' in our lives and, instead, be people who show love, care and forgiveness. When we realise that we have any of these wrong things in our lives, we need to ask God both to forgive us and to help us stop doing wrong. However, we also need to 'throw away' the wrong things—to make a decision that, with God's help, we are not going to do them any more. For example, if we are always gossiping about other people, we will ask God to forgive us and help us, but we will also walk away from conversations when we know we are likely to gossip: we will 'throw away' the opportunity to gossip.

Ask the volunteers who are holding the rubbish to move forward one at a time and throw the rubbish in the bin. As they do so, read the verses again: 'Therefore rid yourself of lies (falsehood), stop stealing, get rid of bitterness, rage, anger, slander, unwholesome talk, malice, filthy language, deceit, envy, hypocrisy, gossip. Instead be kind and compassionate to one another, forgiving each other, just as in Christ God forgave you.'

Challenge

Ask the congregation to close their eyes for a moment and think about today's message. Ask them if they struggle in their own lives with the types of 'rubbish' that have just been thrown in the bin, and challenge them to 'throw them away' now. Challenge them to ask for God's forgiveness and help as they make the decision to walk away next time they are tempted to take part in any of the 'rubbish' on the list.

APPENDIX OF LECTIONARY LINKS

Week 2 (Epiphany)

- Evening Prayer on the Eve (Years A, B, C): Psalms 96 and 97; Isaiah 49:1–13; John 4:7–26

- Principal Service (Years A, B, C): Isaiah 60:1–6; Psalm 72:[1–9]10–15; Ephesians 3:1–12; Matthew 2:1–12

- Second Service (Years A, B, C): Isaiah 60:1–9; John 2:1–11; Evening Psalms 98 and 100

- Third Service (Years A, B, C): Jeremiah 31:7–14; John 1:29–34; Morning Psalms 132 and 113

Week 6 (The Presentation of Christ in the Temple, or Candlemas)

- Evening Prayer on the Eve (Years A, B, C): Psalm 118; 1 Samuel 1:19b–28; Hebrews 4:11–16

- Principal Service (Years A, B, C): Malachi 3:1–5; Psalm 24:[1–6]7–10; Hebrews 2:14–18; Luke 2:22–40

- Second Service (Years A, B, C): Haggai 2:1–9; John 2:18–22; Evening Psalms 122 and 132

- Third Service (Years A, B, C): Exodus 13:1–16; Romans 12:1–5; Morning Psalms 48 and 146

A connection can be made with Saint Thérèse, whose life is remembered on 1 October.

Week 10 (First Sunday in Lent)

Please note that each Sunday in Lent has separate Lectionary readings.

Year A

- Principal Service: Genesis 2:15–17; 3:1–7; Psalm 32; Romans 5:12–19; Matthew 4:1–11
- Second Service: Psalm 50:1–15; Deuteronomy 6:4–9, 16–25; Luke 15:1–10
- Third Service: Psalm 119:1–16; Jeremiah 18:1–11; Luke 18:9–14

Year B

- Principal Service: Genesis 9:8–17; Psalm 25:1–9; 1 Peter 3:18–22; Mark 1:9–15
- Second Service: Psalm 119:17–32; Genesis 2:15–17; 3:1–7; Romans 5:12–19 or Luke 13:31–35
- Third Service: Psalm 77; Exodus 34:1–10; Romans 10:8b–13

Year C

- Principal Service: Deuteronomy 26:1–11; Psalm 91:1–2, 9–16; Romans 10:8b–13; Luke 4:1–13
- Second Service: Psalm 119:73–88; Jonah 3; Luke 18:9–14
- Third Service: Psalm 50:1–15; Micah 6:1–8; Luke 5:27–39

Week 14 (Palm Sunday)

Year A

- Principal Service (Liturgy of the Palms): Matthew 21:1–11; Psalm 118:1–2, 19–29
- Principal Service (Liturgy of the Passion): Isaiah 50:4–9a; Psalm 31:9–16; Philippians 2:5–11; Matthew 26:14—27:66 or Matthew 27:11–54
- Second Service: Psalm 80; Isaiah 5:1–7; Matthew 21:33–46
- Third Service: Psalms 61 and 62; Zechariah 9:9–12; Luke 16:19–31

Year B

- Principal Service (Liturgy of the Palms): Mark 11:1–11 or John 12:12–16; Psalm 118:1–2, 19–24
- Principal Service (Liturgy of the Passion): Isaiah 50:4–9a; Psalm 31:9–16; Philippians 2:5–11; Mark 14:1—15:47 or Mark 15:1–39[40–47]
- Second Service: Psalm 69:1–20; Isaiah 5:1–7; Mark 12:1–12
- Third Service: Psalms 61 and 62; Zechariah 9:9–12; 1 Corinthians 2:1–12

Year C

- Principal Service (Liturgy of the Palms): Luke 19:28–40; Psalm 118:1–2, 19–29

- Principal Service (Liturgy of the Passion): Isaiah 50:4–9a; Psalm 31:9–16; Philippians 2:5–11; Luke 22:14—23:56 or Luke 23:1–49

- Second Service: Psalm 69:1–20; Isaiah 5:1–7; Luke 20:9–19

- Third Service: Psalms 61 and 62; Zechariah 9:9–12; 1 Corinthians 2:1–12

Week 15 (Easter Day)

The reading from Acts must be used as either the first or second reading.

Year A

- Principal Service: Acts 10:34–43 or Jeremiah 31:1–6; Psalm 118:1–2, 14–24; Colossians 3:1–4 or Acts 10:34–43; John 20:1–18 or Matthew 28:1–10

- Second Service: Song of Solomon 3:2–5; 8:6–7; John 20:11–18 if not used at the Principal Service or Revelation 1:12–18; Evening Psalm 105 or 66:1–11

- Third Service: Exodus 14:10–18, 26—15:2; Revelation 15:2–4; Morning Psalms 114 and 117

Year B

- Principal Service: Acts 10:34–43 or Isaiah 25:6–9; Psalm 118:1–2, 14–24; 1 Corinthians 15:1–11 or Acts 10:34–43; John 20:1–18 or Mark 16:1–8

- Second Service: Ezekiel 37:1–14; Luke 24:13–35; Evening Psalm 105 or 66:1–11
- Third Service: Genesis 1:1–5, 26–31; 2 Corinthians 5:14—6:2; Morning Psalms 114 and 117

Year C

- Principal Service: Acts 10:34–43 or Isaiah 65:17–25; Psalm 118:1–2, 14–24; 1 Corinthians 15:19–26 or Acts 10:34–43; John 20:1–18 or Luke 24:1–12
- Second Service: Isaiah 43:1–21; 1 Corinthians 15:1–11 or John 20:19–23; Evening Psalm 105 or 66:1–11
- Third Service: Ezekiel 47:1–12; John 2:13–22; Morning Psalms 114 and 117

Week 19 (Ascension Day)

The reading from Acts must be used as either the first or second reading.

Year A

- Evening Prayer on the Eve: Psalms 15 and 24; 2 Samuel 23:1–5; Colossians 2:20—3:4
- Principal Service: Acts 1:1–11 or Daniel 7:9–14; Psalm 47 or 93; Ephesians 1:15–23 or Acts 1:1–11; Luke 24:44–53
- Second Service: 2 Kings 2:1–15; Revelation 5; Mark 16:14–20 (Gospel at Holy Communion); Evening Psalm 8

- Third Service: Isaiah 52:7–15; Hebrews 7:[11–25]26–28; Morning Psalm 110

Year B

- Evening Prayer on the Eve: Psalms 15 and 24; 2 Samuel 23:1–5; Colossians 2:20—3:4
- Principal Service: Acts 1:1–11 or Daniel 7:9–14; Psalm 47 or 93; Ephesians 1:15–23 or Acts 1:1–11; Luke 24:44–53
- Second Service: 2 Kings 2:1–15; Revelation 5; Matthew 28:16–20 (Gospel at Holy Communion); Evening Psalm 8
- Third Service: Isaiah 52:7–15; Hebrews 7:[11–25]26–28; Morning Psalm 110

Year C

- Evening Prayer on the Eve: Psalms 15 and 24; 2 Samuel 23:1–5; Colossians 2:20—3:4
- Principal Service: Acts 1:1–11 or Daniel 7:9–14; Psalm 47 or 93; Ephesians 1:15–23 or Acts 1:1–11; Luke 24:44–53
- Second Service: 2 Kings 2:1–15; Revelation 5; Matthew 28:16–20 (Gospel at Holy Communion); Evening Psalm 8
- Third Service: Isaiah 52:7–15; Hebrews 7:[11–25]26–28; Morning Psalm 110

Week 22 (Day of Pentecost)

The reading from Acts must be used as either the first or second reading

Year A

- Evening Prayer on the Eve: Psalm 48; Deuteronomy 16:9–15; John 15:26—16:15
- Principal Service: Acts 2:1–21 or Numbers 11:24–30; Psalm 104:26–36, 37b; 1 Corinthians 12:3b–13 or Acts 2:1–21; John 20:19–23 or John 7:37–39
- Second Service: Joel 2:21–32; Acts 2:14–21[22–38]; Luke 24:44–53 (Gospel at Holy Communion); Evening Psalms 67 and 133
- Third Service: Genesis 11:1–9; Acts 10:34–48; Morning Psalm 87

Year B

- Evening Prayer on the Eve: Psalm 48; Deuteronomy 16:9–15; John 7:37–39
- Principal Service: Acts 2:1–21 or Ezekiel 37:1–14; Psalm 104:26–36, 37b; Romans 8:22–27 or Acts 2:1–21; John 15:26–27; 16:4b–15
- Second Service: Ezekiel 36:22–28; Acts 2:22–38; John 20:19–23 (Gospel at Holy Communion); Evening Psalm 139:1–11[13–18, 23–24]
- Third Service: Isaiah 11:1–9; 1 Corinthians 12:4–13; Morning Psalm 145

Year C

- Evening Prayer on the Eve: Psalm 48; Deuteronomy 16:9–15; John 7:37–39
- Principal Service: Acts 2:1–21 or Genesis 11:1–9; Psalm 104:26–36, 37b; Romans 8:14–17 or Acts 2:1–21; John 14:8–17[25–27]
- Second Service: Exodus 33:7–20; 2 Corinthians 3:4–18; John 16:4b–15 (Gospel at Holy Communion); Evening Psalm 33:1–12
- Third Service: Isaiah 40:12–23; 1 Corinthians 2:6–16; Morning Psalms 36:5–10; 150

Week 40 (Bible Sunday)

Year A

- Principal Service: Nehemiah 8:1–4a[5–6]8–12; Psalm 119:9–16; Colossians 3:12–17; Matthew 24:30–35
- Second Service: Psalm 119:89–104; Isaiah 55:1–11; Luke 4:14–30
- Third Service: Psalm 119:137–152; Deuteronomy 17:14–15, 18–20; John 5:36b–47

Year B

- Principal Service: Isaiah 55:1–11; Psalm 19:7–14; 2 Timothy 3:14—4:5; John 5:36b–47

- Second Service: Psalm 119:1–16; 2 Kings 22; Colossians 3:12–17; Luke 4:14–30 (Gospel at Holy Communion)
- Third Service: Psalm 119:89–104; Isaiah 45:22–25; Matthew 24:30–35 or Luke 14:1–14

Year C

- Principal Service: Isaiah 45:22–25; Psalm 119:129–136; Romans 15:1–6; Luke 4:16–24
- Second Service: Psalm 119:1–16; Jeremiah 36:9–32; Romans 10:5–17; Matthew 22:34–40 (Gospel at Holy Communion)
- Third Service: Psalm 119:105–128; 1 Kings 22:1–17; Romans 15:4–13 or Luke 14:1–14

Week 43 (Harvest Thanksgiving)

- Year A: Deuteronomy 8:7–18 or 28:1–14; Psalm 65; 2 Corinthians 9:6–15; Luke 12:16–30 or 17:11–19
- Year B: Joel 2:21–27; Psalm 126; 1 Timothy 2:1–7 or 6:6–10; Matthew 6:25–33
- Year C: Deuteronomy 26:1–11; Psalm 100; Philippians 4:4–9 or Revelation 14:14–18; John 6:25–35

Week 45 (All Saints Day)

Year A

- Evening Prayer on the Eve: Psalms 1 and 5; Isaiah 40:27–31; Revelation 19:6–10
- Principal Service: Revelation 7:9–17; Psalm 34:1–10; 1 John 3:1–3; Matthew 5:1–12
- Second Service: Isaiah 65:17–25; Hebrews 11:32—12:2; Evening Psalms 148 and 150
- Third Service: Isaiah 35:1–9; Luke 9:18–27; Morning Psalms 15, 84 and 149

Year B

- Evening Prayer on the Eve: Psalms 1 and 5; Isaiah 40:27–31; Revelation 19:6–10
- Principal Service: Isaiah 25:6–9; Psalm 24:1–6; Revelation 21:1–6a; John 11:32–44
- Second Service: Isaiah 65:17–25; Hebrews 11:32—12:2; Evening Psalms 148 and 150
- Third Service: Isaiah 35:1–9; Luke 9:18–27; Morning Psalms 15, 84 and 149

Year C

- Evening Prayer on the Eve: Psalms 1 and 5; Isaiah 40:27–31; Revelation 19:6–10

- Principal Service: Daniel 7:1–3, 15–18; Psalm 149; Ephesians 1:11–23; Luke 6:20–31
- Second Service: Isaiah 65:17–25; Hebrews 11:32—12:2; Evening Psalms 148 and 150
- Third Service: Isaiah 35:1–9; Luke 9:18–27; Morning Psalms 15, 84 and 149

Week 48 (First Sunday of Advent)

Year A

- Principal Service: Isaiah 2:1–5; Psalm 122; Romans 13:11–14; Matthew 24:36–44
- Second Service: Psalm 9; Isaiah 52:1–12; Matthew 24:15–28
- Third Service: Psalm 44; Micah 4:1–7; 1 Thessalonians 5:1–11

Year B

- Principal Service: Isaiah 64:1–9; Psalm 80:1–8, 18–20; 1 Corinthians 1:3–9; Mark 13:24–37
- Second Service: Psalm 25; Isaiah 1:1–20; Matthew 21:1–13
- Third Service: Psalm 44; Isaiah 2:1–5; Luke 12:35–48

Year C

- Principal Service: Jeremiah 33:14–16; Psalm 25:1–9; 1 Thessalonians 3:9–13; Luke 21:25–36
- Second Service: Psalm 9; Joel 3:9–21; Revelation 14:13—15:4; John 3:1–17 (Gospel at Holy Communion)
- Third Service: Psalm 44; Isaiah 51:4–11; Romans 13:11–14

Week 51 (Christmas Day)

These sets of readings can be used on Christmas Night or Christmas Day.

Year A

- Principal Service: Isaiah 9:2–7; Psalm 96; Titus 2:11–14; Luke 2:1–14[15–20]
- Second Service: Isaiah 65:17–25; Philippians 2:5–11 or Luke 2:1–20 (if not used in the Principal Service); Evening Psalm 8
- Third Service: Isaiah 62:1–5; Matthew 1:18–25; Morning Psalms 110 and 117

Year B

- Principal Service: Isaiah 62:6–12; Psalm 97; Titus 3:4–7; Luke 2:[1–7]8–20
- Second Service: Isaiah 65:17–25; Philippians 2:5–11 or Luke 2:1–20 (if not used in the Principal Service); Evening Psalm 8

- Third Service: Isaiah 62:1–5; Matthew 1:18–25; Morning Psalms 110 and 117

Year C

- Principal Service: Isaiah 52:7–10; Psalm 98; Hebrews 1:1–4[5–12]; John 1:1–14
- Second Service: Isaiah 65:17–25; Philippians 2:5–11 or Luke 2:1–20 (if not used in the Principal Service); Evening Psalm 8
- Third Service: Isaiah 62:1–5; Matthew 1:18–25; Morning Psalms 110 and 117

IF YOU ENJOYED THIS BOOK YOU MAY LIKE OUR OTHER TITLES:

FILL THE GAP!

120 instant Bible games for
Sunday schools and midweek groups

Ideal for 4–11s

Rebecca Parkinson
Foreword by Roy Crowne, Executive Director, HOPE

ISBN 978 0 85746 004 2
£8.99
240pp

Celebrating Festivals

Readings, reflections, crafts and prayer
activities for 20 major church festivals

Sally Welch

Ideal for use with all ages

ISBN 978 1 84101 711 2

£8.99

224pp

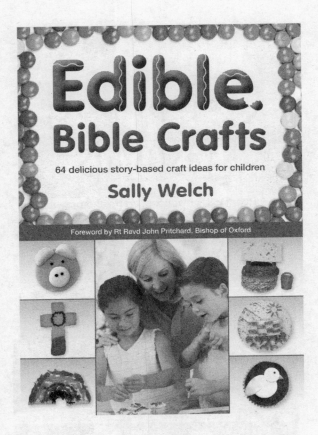

Edible. Bible Crafts

64 delicious story-based craft ideas for children

Sally Welch

Foreword by Rt Revd John Pritchard, Bishop of Oxford

ISBN 978 0 85746 243 5
£11.99
128pp

CREATIVE WORSHIP

20 Bible-based
service outlines
for all-age church

JOHN GUEST

Foreword by Martin Cavender,
Director of ReSource

ISBN 978 0 85746 165 0
£7.99
144pp

Let's Get Together!

Flexible fun-filled activity ideas
for the whole church family

Sue Langwade

One-off specials • Midweek events • Holiday programmes
Away days • Sunday worship • Churches Together initiatives

Foreword by Mark and Helen Johnson, founders of Out of the Ark Music

ISBN 978 1 84101 884 3

£8.99

144pp

More Creative Mission

Over 40 further ideas to help church and community celebrate special days and events throughout the year

Rona Orme

Foreword by Barry Hill, Mission Enabler for the Diocese of Leicester

ISBN 978 0 85746 148 3

£8.99

208pp

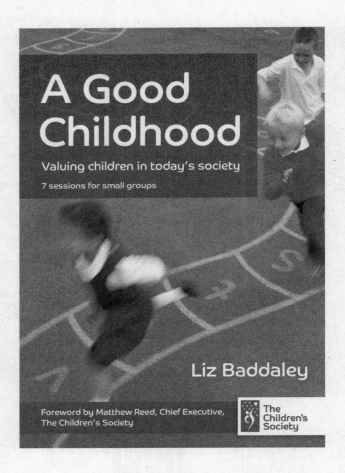

A Good Childhood

Valuing children in today's society

7 sessions for small groups

Liz Baddaley

Foreword by Matthew Reed, Chief Executive,
The Children's Society

The Children's Society

ISBN 978 0 85746 146 9
£7.99
96pp

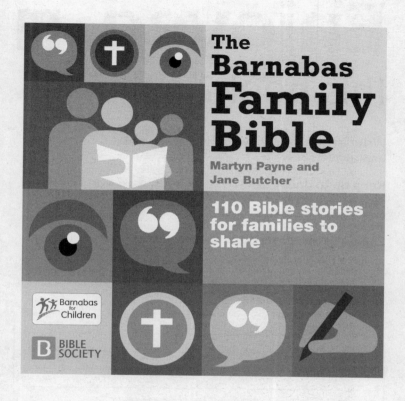

ISBN 978 1 84101 713 6

£9.99

256pp

Enjoyed

this book?

Write a review—we'd love to hear what you think.
Email: reviews@brf.org.uk

Keep up to date—receive details of our new books as they happen.
Sign up for email news and select your interest groups at:
www.brfonline.org.uk/findoutmore/

Follow us on Twitter @brfonline

By post—to receive new title information by post (UK only), complete the form below and post to: BRF Mailing Lists, 15 The Chambers, Vineyard, Abingdon, Oxfordshire, OX14 3FE

Your Details
Name _____
Address_____
_____
Town/City _____ Post Code _____
Email_____

Your Interest Groups (*Please tick as appropriate)	
☐ Advent/Lent	☐ Messy Church
☐ Bible Reading & Study	☐ Pastoral
☐ Children's Books	☐ Prayer & Spirituality
☐ Discipleship	☐ Resources for Children's Church
☐ Leadership	☐ Resources for Schools

Support your local bookshop
Ask about their new title information schemes.